# INFINITE SCALE

How to scale your MSP, be more profitable and regain control of your time

# JAMES VICKERY

'Working with James and the Benchmark 365 team has transformed my relationship with my business. I've been able to disconnect from the day-to-day vortex that was consuming my time and energy, and focus more on my company.'

**Jeremy Johnson, Director, Go Computers**


'Insightful, accomplished, and bold, James Vickery clearly enjoys shaking up the MSP paradigm. Unlike advice from someone who theorizes, his experience running a successful MSP results in thought-provoking and relevant advice. We believe James is a rising star among MSP adviser-experts and our work together helps us take it to the next level!'

**Sheila Bixler and Patrick Beemer, Managing Partners, New Frontier Technologies**


'Working with James Vickery has allowed me to gain more time to build on the relationship with existing clients while also being able to take on more clients. James also provided guidance on converting on-demand clients into block hours – 12 months later and we have literally doubled our revenue and still maintained an excellent profit margin (and all of our clients). Looking forward to the next 12 months with James and the team at Benchmark 365.'

**Junior Soliano, Computer Troubleshooters**

'I've had the pleasure of working with James for more than a year. His knowledge, experience and sage advice has been instrumental in building a solid foundation for my business. Whether it's from a perspective of systems, processes, technology or even sales, James has already been there and done that – and he has been willing to share the knowledge, something that I appreciate immensely. If you run an MSP or are thinking about starting one, I highly recommend getting in touch with James. His willingness to share his experience will save you a *lot* of time, as well as opening your eyes to new ways of doing things, and, critically, creating more revenue!'

**Hayden Burt, Evisent**

First published in 2018 by Benchmark 365

© James Vickery 2018

The moral rights of the author have been asserted

All rights reserved. Except as permitted under the *Australian Copyright Act 1968* (for example, a fair dealing for the purposes of study, research, criticism or review), no part of this book may be reproduced, stored in a retrieval system, communicated or transmitted in any form or by any means without prior written permission.

All inquiries should be made to the author.

A catalogue entry for this book is available from the National Library of Australia.

ISBN: 978-0-6484024-0-4
Project management and text design by Michael Hanrahan Publishing
Cover design by Peter Reardon

**Disclaimer**

The material in this publication is of the nature of general comment only, and does not represent professional advice. It is not intended to provide specific guidance for particular circumstances and it should not be relied on as the basis for any decision to take action or not take action on any matter which it covers. Readers should obtain professional advice where appropriate, before making any such decision. To the maximum extent permitted by law, the author and publisher disclaim all responsibility and liability to any person, arising directly or indirectly from any person taking or not taking action based on the information in this publication.

# CONTENTS

**Preface 1**
　The numbers in perspective　4
　Gratitude　5

**1. Welcome to the whole planet　7**
　The Information Technology sector　7
　More than just IT　9
　The four phases of IT　10
　A false sense of security　11
　A generational threat　12
　Global threats　14
　Do you want to be the cheapest or the best?　16
　'Do you want to catch up for a drink?'　18

**2. The magic box　21**
　My Eureka moment　22
　A typical player in the MSP space　26

**3. Filling your leaky bucket　35**
　The 80/20 rule　36
　Outsourcing　38
　Ramping it up　39
　The leaky bucket syndrome　40
　Only paying for what you use　44

## 4. How scaling up helps you land the big deals  49
Why scaling is important   49
Landing the big deals   52
Scale up but maintain the relationships   54
Embracing the change   58

## 5. Getting rhythm in your business  61
The difficulties of part-time staff   61
When you should insource   63
Workers are being exploited … in Western countries   65
Small business heroics   67
Outsourcing options   69

## 6. Outsourcing the noise and the repeatable stuff  77
So what can you outsource?   78
International outsourcing has come a long way   80
Customers now want an instant fix   81
Tracking your progress   84

## 7. Taking total control of your day  87
Imagine that   87
Giving your customers something to talk about   89
You're a leader, not a tech   90
Getting help   94

## 8. The Benchmark 365 Way    97

Fix the inconsistencies    99
Get a mirror that works    99
Fill those delivery gaps    101
No borders    102
The Benchmark 365 Way in action    103
How can you find out more about Benchmark 365?    110
'Go to Europe – we will run your business.'    111
You got this!    113

## Case study: Infinite Edge gets infinite scale    115

The challenges    115
A turning point    116
Partnering with experience    117
A turnkey approach    117
Better customer experiences    118
Sustainable, healthy profit    119
A Cloud service for people    120

## Case study: Evisent MSP amps up    123

A fresh approach    124
The challenges    124
A unique solution    125
Going live    126
Better customer experiences    126
On-demand MSP expertise    127
Amped up for growth    128

# PREFACE

**I love this industry.** Of all the businesses I could imagine starting there are some very compelling reasons to become and remain an MSP. Where other sectors seem to struggle to adapt to new technology, we are always at the forefront and therefore always have an edge to generate new business opportunities. And whether we start up in a town with three other MSPs or in a city with 3000 of them, we as an industry have always shared an openness to work together to communicate ideas and support one another through the myriad difficulties that MSPs face.

There is truly nothing like this level of collaboration in any other part of the business community.

It's in the spirit of this openness and sharing that I had always wanted to write a book, ever since starting my IT company 'I Know IT' back in 2003.

There was just one problem that perhaps you can relate to: I never had any time! Like many in our industry I'd spent the better part of my career as an MSP owner putting out fires, whether they be customer outages ruining my weekend, hiring, training, losing and managing staff, finance and cash flow concerns limiting our growth, or difficult customers with relentless demands. All of this before spending a moment on marketing and sales in order to actually grow the company instead of just keeping the lights on.

These issues consumed me for more than a decade, until I finally got things under control and got the company scaled up.

It's funny, but the very reason I was drawn to the idea of launching an MSP was this concept of having everything automated. The holy grail of work happening behind the scenes while I traveled the world from one tropical location to another with little to no input from me is something I believed would be accomplished in a few short years.

But more than a decade into running I Know IT, I became conscious that fully automating this business was a dichotomy. I also believe this to be true for all MSPs in the market today. Sure, there are a ton of great automation software products you can buy and many talented developers and respected vendors behind them, but the fact still remains that running an MSP requires people. People to talk to customers, people to step in when the automation cannot, people to be on call late at night, and people to interpret the needs of those who have no desire to be IT experts and just want someone else to handle it all for them so they, like you, can accomplish their goals.

Therefore, this *isn't* a book about technology. There are plenty of forums, books, podcasts, events and conferences that can answer all the IT questions you can think up. Instead, this is a book about transforming your mindset and getting your business under control. It's a book about scaling up now so you can take advantage of the tremendous and limitless opportunities out there for you.

Writing this book has coincided with the truly unexpected rapid growth of our company Benchmark 365. What an incredible journey. At the time that I started *Infinite Scale*, Benchmark 365 was a small Australian and Philippines company with a select group of Aussie MSPs, who we refer to as Pilot Partners. We made a mutual investment in one another with a simply stated yet ambitious goal: if we put all of our 15 years of experience, all of our resources, all of our best people, all of our expertise and all of our knowledge behind an MSP, can we make them grow profitably and successfully? Can we make them beat the market odds in terms of financial performance, and can we help the often overwhelmed owner take back their life and take back control?

The result was more than we – and I suspect they – could have ever imagined as we witnessed several of these partners double or triple in revenue in less than a year with substantially higher profitability. As word spread, we found ourselves a not-so-little company anymore, with MSP partners in the US, Canada and the UK in addition to our incredible Australian partners.

With so much growth comes so many learnings, and even as this book is wrapped up and sent to the publisher I can already envision a second edition. With the same spirit of openness and collaboration that we all value in this industry, I encourage you to keep up to date by visiting our blog from time to time. Myself and the team will share any learnings we've had and keep our community informed. You can check it out at www.benchmark365.com.

## The numbers in perspective

This book is all about scaling up profitably.

Despite the passion that many have for one pricing model over another, the fact is that there is more than one way to make money as an IT business and there is more than one way to price and deliver your services.

I've had the pleasure of meeting very wealthy 'break–fix' business owners who have gone against all the industry advice and stuck with hourly rate servicing. I've also met staggeringly successful fixed-fee MSPs who are charging 4× the market average seat or device price and are doing extremely well too.

Throughout this book I'll use examples that discuss hourly rates and fixed fees interchangeably. These are just that – examples to help you reflect on your own circumstances and run your own numbers.

The prescription and essence of this book isn't how to package your pricing, it's how to make sure every second of work you do for your client is profitable and delivered in the most cost-effective way. MSPs who understand their numbers can get very creative and very clever with pricing because they know exactly what it costs to deliver their service every ticket, every minute and every day.

## Gratitude

Business can be a lonely game. As it turns out, so can writing a book! I am very grateful to those who have helped keep me sane and on track for over a year while I put this together. Whether it's my wonderful wife Janice who has juggled our newborn son Redmond while entertaining our two older boys James and Alex (also referred to as 'seek and destroy'), while I hammered away at the keyboard late at night and on weekends. Where would I be without you? Or whether it's my good friend and colleague Andrew, who encouraged me to write it in the first place and helped shape its direction. Or our marketing superstar Patrick who has been instrumental in editing and making suggestions, and has a true gift for helping me articulate my story and my beliefs.

Thank you, thank you, thank you.

And of course a shout out to our incredible Benchmark 365 team who work tirelessly for our partners night and day. Strength and Honor.

And to you – the MSP who wants to either start or grow and scale your business profitably. Thank you for reading this book. I hope it gives you the ideas and the motivation to do what it takes to grow your business and accomplish your dreams.

*To your success,*

*JV*

# 1. WELCOME TO THE WHOLE PLANET

> My MSP business doubled in size once I figured out this stuff, and it has doubled in size year on year for the last five years.

**Outsourcing is an important** business strategy, especially for growing businesses, and I am confident that the principles behind my advice are broad enough to be applied to almost any sector and any small to medium-sized enterprise. However, the sector I am particularly referring to is known as Managed Service Providers, which I will refer to throughout as MSPs. *Infinite Scale* looks like a book about IT, but it's really a book about growing your business, and yourself.

## The Information Technology sector

The current state of the Information Technology (IT) sector is a business paradox. There are two major factors constraining its expansion, yet it's simultaneously showing tremendous signs of growth. Many MSPs fail to achieve revenues beyond $1m per annum, yet the global IT services industry is estimated to be worth a whopping USD$960bn.[1] Contraction or expansion? Which is it? My eyes were opened when I saw a bigger picture. The answer is *solid growth*, but only if done in a cost-effective way. Working through these issues in my business has inspired me to share my conclusions for the benefit of other business owners, because once I figured this stuff out my business doubled in size and has continued to double in size year on year for the last five years. You can grow your business in exactly the same way.

MSP business owners are smart. Some have diplomas, some have postgraduate degrees, yet when you truly look at the numbers and analyze the bottom line, many are earning far less than they deserve, and often less than a plumber or a carpenter. I say to these IT people, 'You deserve to earn more than a plumber! You're qualified, you're a smart person, you've worked hard. For all your years of experience, how do you make less than a tradesperson?'

Managed Service Providers are doing it tough, often sitting up extra-late trying to keep some small business client functioning online. It's hard on them. They're exhausted. They have to be available 24 hours a day. They're glued to their phone, and their partner is screaming, 'If you don't sort out your business issues, I'm out!' I reckon, if MSPs are going through all that stress and angst, they need to earn good money, otherwise what's the point? At least

---

[1] www.gartner.com/newsroom/id/3871063

working for someone else as an employee is usually limited to 9 to 5.

The challenges in our industry are both a blessing and a curse. One blessing is that you don't need a lot of capital to start an MSP. Anybody who has a few IT skills can create a LinkedIn account, launch a website and begin 'virtually' knocking on doors. The Internet is ubiquitous. There is no barrier to entry. You don't even need a diploma – although I hasten to add, I think it helps. Anyone can get online, send an email, target a customer, and say, 'I'll do your IT for half the price of your current IT provider'.

## More than just IT

Accountants, lawyers and financial planners are seen as trusted business advisers. I'm proposing that your technology expertise puts you on the same level. Being an IT expert puts you at the forefront of ideas to help your customers grow. That's what makes you a trusted adviser.

The IT space is very large and very broad. There are certain disciplines and specializations. Maybe you are very good at cyber-security, protecting client networks from being hacked, or even destroyed. You may be very good at helping companies with their productivity. Others are more technical and have deep expertise in networking or voice over IP. There are different learning paths for each, and different tracks you can go on. The more competencies you have the more confidence you have, which allows you to target more companies or even bigger companies, helping you to grow your revenue. It's good to keep learning because this is one industry that's constantly on the move.

## The four phases of IT

In the 15 years I've been in the IT business we've been through quite a few shifts. I've divided them into four different phases:

1   **Break–fix.** *Simple and straightforward.* I started with a screwdriver and an idea; that *was* the first phase, and it was how things were 15 years ago. A small business would call me up and say, 'James, my computer's broken…' and I'd say, 'Okay, I'll fix it and I'll charge you $100'. A week later they would phone up and say the printer doesn't work, and I'd charge another $100, which is why I call that the break–fix stage. Big disadvantage: unpredictable revenue and cash flow.

2   **Managed Service Provider (MSP).** *Taking care of business.* When the industry started to mature, companies wanted to fix their costs so their accountants and everyone else knew where they stood financially. It also helped the service providers, giving them a retainer that enabled them to budget too. These companies were saying, 'I don't want to pay by the hour for IT support, I want you to tell me how much it's going to cost me every month for you to maintain my company's entire system'. From that, the managed services industry evolved, which is where most of the readers of this book will be right now.

3   **The Cloud.** *The ultimate in de-centralization.* Then came a burst in Internet information services. There wasn't anything you couldn't find out and there wasn't anything you couldn't buy online. In fact, a lot of information came free, and everything moved to the Cloud. It went from hands-on computer servicing to customers suddenly saying, 'We don't need software on our computers any more, we just go online, sign in and it's all there…so, what do you guys actually do for me now?'

4   **Open for business.** *Welcome to the whole planet.* As I write, we are in a fourth phase where globalisation has turned service into a mixture of in-house and offshore labor. You and your clients are not simply competing with the MSP across the street. Anybody can go after your customers. And so MSP businesses need to be far more agile than they ever were.

The technology is going to keep moving more and more radically; the one thing that hasn't changed is that *we still don't understand where it will all end.* We've survived three phases, we're living in a fourth, and there will be a fifth phase and a sixth. One day there'll be a tenth phase! We all need to keep moving.

## A false sense of security

Over the past decade some of the smaller IT providers have climbed to $1 million per year in revenue, so they're feeling pretty good about their businesses. I'm not suggesting they've been hugely profitable, but many see $1 million in annual revenue as the Holy Grail and many have set their sights on achieving revenues at this level. Some have made it, but now comes a shift in the axis. A loyal client says to you, 'You've been doing a great job for us over the last 10 years, but I'm out – see you later'. All of a sudden that $1 million is reduced to $950,000 or $900,000. It may not seem like much, and it may seem like an anomaly – but it's actually a trend. The industry is constantly changing. Companies are no longer buying traditional on-premises technology – they're buying software online, and so MSPs who aren't embracing this change and helping their customers make informed decisions will have less to manage than they ever did before.

## A generational threat

I still have some of my original clients from when I started all those years ago. When we started working together the proprietors were in their late 30s. They were owner-operators who ran their own small businesses, like screen-printing, law or small manufacturing, and when they struck an IT problem they would phone me and say, 'James, I don't understand IT, can you come in and fix it?' Many have stayed with me for 15 years. However, 30% of my MSPs clients have sold their businesses over the last two years. The older ones – those who signed with me when they were 45 to 50 years old – are saying, 'I'm 60 (or 65) and I'm out.'

## 1. Welcome to the whole planet

Those people are now coming up for retirement, and the issue of succession keeps arising. Like many successful businesses, their kids inherit the operation, so Millennial kids are coming in and running the family business. They have never known a world without computers; they probably had an iPhone when they were in school. Now they're going, 'What exactly do you do for my parents?' And you – or I – explain to these Millennials how you keep the IT system running, only to have them reply, 'I know how all this technology works. I'm not fazed by this kind of stuff. You've been a good friend to my parents and I wish we could still use your services, but there's nothing you have to offer that we can't easily deal with ourselves. Sorry.' This is a threat if MSPs don't adapt and change their value proposition. These new breed of business owners are much bigger consumers of IT so the opportunity is still there, but not if you try to sell to them the way you might have sold to their parents.

We've got a generational threat, because while they may appreciate your loyalty over the years, change is afoot. They may even have sold the business to another group that has an in-house IT department and they no longer need outside support. So there are two similar threats: they've either consolidated, or a Millennial kid has taken over the maintenance of their computers and moved everything online. They pick up the phone, call their MSP, and announce, 'We've got this great new app that does everything and we don't need you anymore'. That's a huge threat to small MSP companies – which is where we come in to help (more on this later).

Millennials buy technology differently than their parents did, and they will adopt different IT policies. When I started my business 15 years ago there was a price for supplying IT services. It was either an hourly rate or a monthly fee charged per device or per user. That price has not gone up; in fact, that price – in a lot of circumstances – has gone *down*. At the same time, the cost of staffing has increased in all Western markets (US, Canada, Australia, UK, NZ, etc.). Wages have not gone down, they've gone up. So you're having to deliver more for less. It's not unique to our industry – it's a threat in all service industries.

So technology is changing, Millennials are entering the market, and the cost of labor is rising, but the biggest threat of all is competition. More and more IT businesses are starting up every day, *all over the planet*.

## Global threats

In theory, I can work from anywhere. I could get my laptop out and run my IT business from a café in the south of France. I could log into my clients' computers and deal with their problems while sipping coffee – and that sounds great, right? So a lot of people in managed services boast, 'I can work from the beach ... I can work from anywhere ... gee I've got a great life!'

What they're not realizing is that *everybody else* in their sector can also service clients anywhere in the world. Their competition used to be a couple of similar businesses in their local neighborhood, but the competition is now

## 1. Welcome to the whole planet

global. Someone like me can target customers in upstate New York, Perth or Toronto. That wasn't happening before, not like this.

Global competition is a threat to your business. Nothing is local any more. You are in competition with thousands of other providers, all around the world. In a low-barrier-to-entry sector, there are more and more businesses doing what you do. Not everyone is content to sit in a picturesque environment and put lifestyle ahead of growth. I'm not saying there's anything wrong with a policy of non-expansion. In fact, it's fantastic if you're happy to have a little lifestyle business where it's just you running the business from a coffee shop or on a beach. But every day I speak with MSPs who say they want to grow, want to scale, want to expand, until they are hands off, making a substantial annual income or being able to sell to a bigger player for serious profit.

> Global competition is a threat to your business. Nothing is local any more. You are in competition with thousands of other providers, all around the world.

Until a few years ago, many small businesses operated with just one server, which was a 'box' where all the records were stored. Some companies had several servers. Their information was centralized on the premises. In these physical premises every staff member had a desk, a phone and a computer. The MSP would approach this business, and say, 'I'm going to manage your server and support you 24 hours a day. I'm going to keep on top of all the IT issues, and I'm going to charge $150 per device or per user per month to manage all that.' That model used to make a lot of sense because there might be a server outage or some other issue that the MSP could solve. So the MSP would come onsite with a laptop or they would dial in from a remote location, make sure the system was back working, and everyone was happy.

Then, this way of working started to disappear.

Instead of putting a server in the office, small to medium businesses have begun to migrate to the Cloud (often assisted by you or another MSP). They have started using Cloud-based accounting software instead of an application on their PC. Everything has changed, and now how they used to operate seems too slow because all the shortcuts on the desktop that used to point to the server room and get processed, icon-by-icon, now point to the Cloud where everything is stored online.

The owners are now saying, 'I'm going to get rid of this clunky old server. I want everything online – and I don't need computer support any more'.

Have a think about what this means for *your* business...

## Do you want to be the cheapest or the best?

The smart MSPs are seeing the next wave of opportunity in disaster prevention, cyber security and business productivity. They aren't walking away: they are extending their role as IT advisers and encouraging clients to retool their businesses. They are helping clients make smart decisions about what they put into the Cloud. They're advising caution, and suggesting strong backups to make sure that data can't be wiped out. If the US Government can get hacked, if Adobe can get hacked, your client's small business can get hacked. There are ways to prevent this from happening, and that's a big opportunity in the industry if that's your area of specialization and you are the trusted adviser.

The relationship in such situations is clear, but the pricing model may need readjustment. The client may not see the value anymore, partly because the client isn't necessarily well informed. She may wonder what she's paying for if all her intellectual property is safely stored in the Cloud. (But is it really safe?) You need to inform your client, keep her abreast of the industry, step up your relationship, sit with her once a month, discuss strategy, find ways to secure the company data, find ways for the staff to be more productive.

The smart MSPs aren't taking their prices down, they're putting their prices up. The misguided ones are dropping their prices, and the industry is going through a radical pricing problem as a result. These uncertain times are causing many MSPs to get worried. They call me for advice. They say, 'I'm having a problem with a client who doesn't want to pay because they don't know what we're doing any more – and I don't want to lose that client'.

I reply, 'When was the last time you saw that client?'

They often sheepishly reply, 'I haven't been out there for months'.

> **The smart MSPs aren't taking their prices down, they're putting their prices up.**

I say, 'Go and have a coffee with him, have a chat about the problem, find out why he doesn't want to pay you. You never know – it just might be a relationship that needs a bit of gardening.'

And they say, 'I'd never thought of that, James!'

It sounds like paradise, sitting in a coffee shop instead of an office going, 'I can work from anywhere'. But in a global marketplace, unless you're maintaining your client relationships, they will eventually look online and say, 'If we're going to deal with faceless companies, I might as well go online and just pick a cheaper one'. And that's where the price becomes a factor, because customers are likely to pay you more simply based on the trust they bestow on you. If it's all about a price war, with clients saying, 'I want you to be the cheapest', you should reply, 'I want to be the best!'

## 'Do you want to catch up for a drink?'

My top 10 customers are the ones with whom I can pick up the phone and say, 'Do you want to catch up for a drink? No reason, I just want to say hi and make sure everything is going okay in your business.' We seldom talk about IT – and year after year they continue to buy more and more from us because I show up.

I was speaking to a great partner – now friend – named Cameron when Cameron was going through a divorce. His MSP was as shaky as his marriage. He had to make staff redundant because he was losing money. I saw him the other day – he took me to a concert. He simply wanted to thank me for what we've done for him. He said, 'I know you're a huge fan of the Foo Fighters, and I've bought tickets to their concert. I'd like you to come along, and I'd like to shout you dinner as well' (even though he's already paying me for my service). We represent so much value to his business that he said, 'James, you saved my business – you saved my life!'

That's because I told him what I've just told you in this chapter, that the IT sector has a thin and alluring veneer – $1 million pa turnover – but with a new generation coming up and worldwide competitors on the horizon, business is beginning to slip.

But one thing they can't ever take away is the client relationship.

Focus on that.

# 2. THE MAGIC BOX

> Some of your employees can earn up to $100,000 a year. They need to deliver more than $100,000 a year to your business, or you're not in business.

**I was really struggling.** We were turning over roughly $1 million pa but we hadn't grown. We were taking on more and more costs. I was employing more and more staff. We were losing a customer here and there, so I had to scramble to catch up again. After 12 years in business, I was employing seven people but our revenue was not growing as expected. Our revenue had been about the same for five years. I was having hassles with staff, who refused to understand that they needed to carefully account for their time so that customers could be billed.

I was having a hard time, when someone said, 'Let's do a business tour around the Philippines…' I thought, *at least I can get out of the office for a few days and clear my mind.* I knew I needed to get away for a while, and the trip could be good for our business.

I got as far as the airport. I was relaxing and having a drink when I received a text message from a customer: 'What the hell's going on? Our server is down!' It was our largest customer, with 40 employees – and their whole system was offline. I said, 'I'm about to get on a plane. Let me call the office – they'll sort it out'.

I called the office. My most senior and trusted Systems Engineer, Alex, was away sick. So there I was, sitting at the airport thinking, 'If I get on this plane, I could lose this customer. This could be a fatal blow to the company…'.

I did what I could for my customer – and I made the decision to get on the plane. It was the hardest flight of my life. Anyone in this position knows what it feels like: *what if the staff don't get the system back online and we lose the customer? What are we going to do? Am I going to go out of business?*

All this fear.

Fear I'm going to go out of business.

Fear my family's going to be living on the street.

Why do I have to feel like this?

But the trip was important – I decided to stick with it.

## My Eureka moment

When I landed I'd received a dozen angry text messages saying, 'Get back here right now!' I could have returned, but I completed my business tour instead and got to see

## 2. The magic box

people doing amazing things. I got to see Australian companies, American companies, European companies, all running very successful operations offshore from a range of industries.

Having an angry client back home made this a very stressful trip. Maybe that's what heightened my curiosity. I was asking myself, *how is it that these Western businesses have made their way up to having 50, 100, 1000 people (one US company had 100,000 employees!) – and why is it that we in the MSP industry are struggling to make a profit, working long hours and fearing the customer calling up while we're trying to take a three-day break?*

The answer was like a lightbulb going off in my head. It was my Eureka moment. It didn't all come to me overnight. I had to give it some thought. But I suddenly decided: I'm going to hire someone right here in the Philippines! On this trip! Just one person.

> It's a game of scale: if I can keep my customers happy because they don't have their system down, we can be better and more successful and everybody's happy.

His name was Mark, and he turned out to be a real asset. Mark took on a lot of the burden that some of my team were not taking on, and my business was paying him a fraction of the amount of what I was paying in Australia.

Mark became a real blessing for us. He was hard working, diligent, and able to do a lot of technical work that we were struggling with. Alex missed more time due to illness, and Mark was able to step in and solve those problems.

Then I started to think, *if I can get Mark for a third of the cost of a local staff member, and Alex keeps letting me down and is costing me so much more, let's just have Mark.* That's the natural progression of thought, right? So the problem of Alex being away sick is solved because Mark is there – and if Mark takes a day off, I need another 'Mark' to be there.

From the experiences that flowed I learned that it's not a game of reducing expenses, it's a game of scale: if I can keep my customers happy because they don't have their system down, we can be better and more successful and everybody's happy.

### 'My computer's not working properly – log in now and fix it'

I made the decision to set up my business in the Philippines in 2012. We now have offices in several locations around the country. One office is in a new building in the middle of town surrounded by the likes of Accenture, IBM and Lexmark, and we have offices in Australia and North America as well. Telecommunications is the main reason we need an office offshore, and we don't use home-based freelance workers. We're doing telephone support for our partners and their customers 24 hours a day, so we need it to be professional at all times.

The first thing people say is, 'What do you do when you need someone to go to their office for onsite support?'

I reply, 'That's 1% of the time' – because if your MSP is set up properly there's no need to cross town and be onsite. That sort of talk reflects the screwdriver mindset. These people say, 'That wouldn't work for me', but I'm telling you it does because we've been doing it now for many years. On the rare occasion we do need someone onsite, we subcontract a local break–fix company, and they cost a fraction of hiring a local employee who would be overpaid and underutilized.

Some people are still starting out with a screwdriver today. They say, 'James did that 15 years ago and he's doing okay. Why don't I do the same and start out with a screwdriver…?' Sorry folks, that's never going to work. That's gone, it's over: customers want to pick up the phone – and sometimes not even that. They want to send an email or open up a chat session and say, 'My computer's not working properly – log in now and fix it'. And they want it *fast*. They want it like this: 'When I call, you better be on this in the next five minutes'.

### You still can't beat local contact

In writing this, I want to be cautious. I don't want to say, go fire a whole lot of people and outsource all your business overseas. I don't want to say that because I don't feel that way. You can't beat local contact and a familiar face. But I do feel my team (and yours) need to climb to the level to justify what they're costing your business. I'm sure they're working right, they're just not billing right!

Some MSP employees earn anywhere from $60,000 to $100,000 a year. So they need to deliver more than $100,000 a year to your business – or you're not in business.

It's not simply having call centers overseas, it's about a combination of positive local experiences and overseas expertise. Deliver more to your customer, give a better outcome, and they're going to keep coming back. That's first base in what happened to make my business grow and become substantially more profitable. My business life changed when I figured out how to fulfill my customers' needs through a combination of offshore MSP teams and local area marketing.

## A typical player in the MSP space

Maybe, like me, you too had a passion for computers as a teenager. And something must have brought you to a realization that there is a place in the workforce for your skills. From there, it's only a short hop to turning it into your 'job', and what a great job – free from the chains of a 9-to-5 working life, avoiding subservience to a boss, and after a few years being well paid. Like me, you probably couldn't believe your luck! Unfortunately, the world has since turned, your profit margins have undoubtedly shrunk, your business is probably not growing, and you're wondering what the heck is going on?

If you've been in the game for more than a decade, I'm certain you will identify with the changes we've all had to face,

## 2. The magic box

and hopefully you will get some value from the ideas in this book. I'm going to share my past because it's the tale of a typical player in the MSP space. Here's my story, so you can see and understand where I'm coming from.

I've never known a world without computers. Mum and Dad bought our first PC when I was eight. This was way before the Internet, and at a time when most kids didn't have access to a home computer. My parents had it for work. Dad wasn't an IT person but he saw the value in having it – he saw opportunities. In those times, the big things were word processing and spreadsheets, but I was mainly interested in games. When my parents went out, they thought I'd be studying or watching TV. They didn't know I was curious about their PC, this magic box. I'd unscrew the back to take a peek at what was inside. They never knew I did this.

I started by removing a couple of screws, then I'd get a bit scared and screw them back in. Then the next time I'd wonder, *what would happen if I took the whole case off?* So I did that, took a good hard look, and tried to deduce how it worked. I wasn't interested in the software or programming. I just liked the hardware.

I was fascinated. I became the computer kid figuring stuff out. I think I was just 'that geek'. Seeing the logic of what was inside the casing gave me a feeling that there must be a way to connect our family computer to other computers. I had certainly heard about modems and that sort of connective technology, so I was curious to know how to get more out of this box, and I got better and better at doing it.

I kept this part of my life secret. I never told my friends that I was pulling computers apart. They wouldn't have been interested anyway. They were only interested in games. We'd buy games and bring them to school on five-and-a-quarter-inch floppy disks, the technology of the time. A friend might say, 'I'd like a copy of that', and I'd go, 'What games have you got?' And we'd swap and copy each other's games.

Then came a dramatic shift in computing, from command-line interface to having a mouse and running Windows. Things started to boom with the launch of Windows 3.1, and then Windows 95. More and more people started to have computers, and a few years later, when I was in my late teens, came dial-up Internet. That's when computing became even more fascinating.

The Internet provided a facility for me to start my own bulletin board service (BBS). People could dial in to me and I could share things – like video games, of course. I could also jump on a chatline and connect with someone on the other side of the country.

### I Know IT

When I was 23, I decided to start a business and call it *I Know IT*. I liked to pull computers apart, which gave me the confidence to feel I was pretty knowledgeable on the subject. I had no business plan, and I didn't have any

## 2. The magic box

money. Most business start-up costs are enormous, but I didn't have to spend any money – all I needed was a screwdriver. I was working from home, living with Mum and Dad in Sydney, Australia.

My main expenditure was to have some business cards printed, after which I called on local businesses and said, 'How about I look after your computers?' I just called door to door on anyone who had an office in my area. I'd walk in, tell them what I was about, and hand over my business card.

I soon learned that they had a lot of problems. We were in the aftermath of the Y2K scare, when everybody was worried that – due to some poor programming in the operating system that most computers used – their computers were going to cease functioning when the calendar clicked over to 2000. So people had bought a bunch of new computers in 1999–2000, in an urgent hurry. They'd been told, 'This'll solve your Y2K problem'. But often they'd been sold dated technology, so I'd go into all these businesses and have to explain, 'You've been ripped off – this has all been wrongly set up', or, 'You need to replace this bit and that bit'. My role was fairly straightforward.

On my third day in business I walked into a small Ray White real estate agency and walked out with $10,000 worth of work. That was a huge amount of money to me, maybe a quarter of what I'd earned a year working in regular employment, so I thought, 'Wow, this is easy money!' I had no idea what I was doing, yet I'd scored $10,000 worth of work on my third day.

However, I'd like to explain that doesn't mean I had pocketed a quick $10,000. The real estate agent needed a couple of new computers, a couple of new monitors, and I had to set everything up properly. By the time I'd bought the parts, done all the labor and all the things that go with that, there wasn't a lot left. Even so, $10,000 was an impressive sum, so I kept on going door to door.

By the time I attracted my third or fourth customer, I called on one of my mates and said, 'Why don't I get you to do this job, and while you're doing that I'll go across there and do this other job – and now I've got a bigger business!' So I had a very strong sense of the benefits of scaling even then. I think I was very lucky to get that education almost from day one.

I acquired 15 customers in a short space of time and ran the business myself, as well as doing most of the tech support. Pretty soon I realised my time was stretched thin.

## My big mistake

After some early successes with I Know IT I finally moved out of home and began running my business from an apartment. One of my customers was in the demolition/construction sector and bought a massive warehouse. He saw my business was growing, and he offered me a hole-in-the-wall office space in exchange for me handling his company's IT. Stupidly, I said yes.

## 2. The magic box

He'd bought this massive space because his business was growing quite rapidly. It started with five staff, which is when I agreed to handle his IT in return for rent-free office space. Then it grew to 20, then 30 employees. Soon my staff was just running around servicing his staff's computers, and I never had any time to grow my business, so it was a pretty great deal for them. That demolition business quickly expanded to 80 people.

### Financially stretched

I did the maths, started to wisen up, and said, 'I really appreciate having free office space, but this is the value of what we're doing for you'. I showed him the figure. We eventually parted ways. I dropped the seemingly free office and put proper contracts in place. The year was 2008, and I rented our first office space. I had five employees – struggle, struggle, struggle – and then the global financial crisis hit. The demolition company went out of business, as did a lot of our customers in those sorts of industries. They were all heavily affected by the GFC.

The common approach around that time was that a customer would call up, talk a problem through, and I'd say, 'I'd better send Alex to visit you onsite'. So Alex would go onsite, disappear for four hours for a one-hour job (on a big salary), and I couldn't get the time entries to justify his time. Eventually I'd send out the bill for four hours, and the customer would say to me, 'James, we're not paying you for four hours, he was only here for one!' That was another blow. So I tried fixed fees.

The new fixed-fee approach came with a guarantee we'd be onsite within the hour, and we'd also guarantee a certain amount of uptime on their system. Financially it was a disaster. My employees couldn't meet those service levels. A lot of MSPs still use this approach, and that's a danger in this industry. They have the staff, but doing it this way, they don't understand that they're probably losing money but they justify it with the belief that the customer is going to buy new hardware some day soon so it should eventually balance out.

Meanwhile, the margin on new computers is now half or less what it was when I started out. You're caught up in the revenue – a bit of money coming in when the customer buys a new computer, a bit more when the customer buys a new printer. You get caught up in all of that, and you don't even have time to look at your costs, and before you know it you're financially stretched and you're the one doing all the work.

You're the one staying up late at night.

You're the one handling all the complaints.

You're the one doing the books and figuring out what's going on in the business. I hope you're not in this position right now.

Every small business seems to suffer this at some stage, or partly suffer this. Even though the numbers look good – it doesn't necessarily translate into profit. Read on if you want to know how to escape – or avoid – this phase.

## Questions to ask yourself

### *What's your Eureka moment?*

Can you think of a recent event or experience with a customer or employee that made you question what in the hell it is you are doing? Perhaps it was a customer having a major IT problem when you're on vacation, or when you're sitting down for a meal with your family.

Remember that feeling and anxiety – and vow to think differently and do what it takes to avoid this happening to you again. Use this moment to drive change in your business.

### *Are you financially stretched?*

Take some time to really study your financial situation. Are you working too hard for the money you are making? Can you account for every minute of your staff's working day? Is it paid for? Do your customers pay for everything you do for them? How much do you do just based on the hope of some future purchase by them?

### *Where do you want to be?*

Thinking about your answers to the previous questions, ask yourself, *where is it that you would like your business to be?* What does your day feel and look like without scrambling or working all hours to a keep customer happy? How would you like to be paid for your services? And of course, what kind of lifestyle can this give you?

# 3. FILLING YOUR LEAKY BUCKET

*If you want to stay strong in business, keep filling your leaky bucket.*

**You're running an MSP** and you want it to grow. You want to hit milestones. You want to get bigger. You want to get to a certain level of turnover. The most important thing you can do is to focus on sales.

At some point MSPs lose customers. Maybe they're buying software elsewhere or buying hardware elsewhere. Maybe they have found cheaper services online, or maybe there's simply more competition. At some point, faithful old customers are going to leave and you've got to scramble to replace them. And if you're not out there filling up this leaky bucket, getting new blood in, you're screwed.

Like every owner-operator, your business has succeeded because you are good at whatever your business produces

– in this instance you're a great technician and you're on the tools. I'm sure you've been working hard and doing it tough. There's much change going on, there's so much threat out there, you've got to keep topping the bucket up, which is why you need to switch your focus from fixing to selling. The best person in the business to do the selling is you, because you're the one who cares the most. You're certain to be good at sales because you never were 'just' a technician – you had to convince customers to climb on board right from the start, otherwise you would never have got this far.

We've benchmarked the industry and found the key difference between small players and the bigger players is sales. If the owner, or the senior person in the business, focuses more than 80% of his or her time on sales, the business grows. But small players spend at least 80% of their time on technology. I want to encourage people reading this book to turn that equation on its head.

> We've benchmarked the industry and found the key difference between small players and the bigger players is sales.

## The 80/20 rule

That 80% figure reminds me of the famous Pareto principle (also known as the 80/20 rule). I'll leave it to you to Google Vilfredo Pareto if you're interested, but one hundred years ago in Italy this social researcher concluded that, for many events, roughly 80% of the effects come from 20% of the causes.

Most things in life are not distributed evenly. The 80/20 rule is a rough guide to typical distributions. It can mean:

- 20% of your work time generates 80% of your growth
- 20% of input creates 80% of the outcome
- 20% of workers produce 80% of the result
- 20% of the customers create 80% of the revenue
- 20% of your product generates 80% of your turnover
- and so it goes…

I'm suggesting that if 80% of your work time is spent on the tools your business will shrink. Conversely, I believe your business will grow if 80% of your time is spent on active and passive selling. Sales is the reason my business grew 100% – nothing else, just sales.

When MSP owners get hit by a client with a technical problem, they rush to deal with it. In doing so they drop the relationship with other clients, focus on some humdrum emergency, and their business contracts just a little more. In fixing the client's problem they have created a problem of their own. A few customers notice the neglect and leave – the bucket leaks – and the owner-operator knows he has to top it up and has a burst on sales, then it's back to fighting fires again. And that's why their businesses don't grow. The simple answer is: get a bigger bucket – which they never do. They keep racing off and giving tech support, which leaves little time for getting more customers. In these businesses, the revenue gradually shrinks over a period of years.

In re-examining your business model, you need to do something about that leaky bucket – customers coming in the top and falling out the bottom. You've got to keep filling up the bucket. Everything I just said is actually critical.

## Outsourcing

One solution is outsourcing, which allows you to focus on what you're *supposed* to be doing, which is growing the business.

Imagine a coffee shop with 100 customers coming through and the owner takes the role of barista, focusing all day on making the coffees and having no spare time to talk to anyone. The coffee would probably be great, but the customer service would not be exemplary. To stretch my IT scenario into the world of coffee shops, I'm suggesting they should hire a barista so the owner's role is to greet customers and make them feel good, and concentrate on the ambiance, a cheerful atmosphere and friendly conversations – whatever it takes for them to look forward to coming back.

I've had the pleasure of meeting the owner of a famous Australian coffee distributor, Vittoria Coffee. Les Shirato operates from premises in Sydney, Australia. He doesn't spend his day making coffee, he's got a business to run!

He's got 250 employees and a revenue figure of $250 million per year. Les makes $1 million per employee per year. Wouldn't it be amazing to see numbers like that in an MSP? I suggest you should be recovering at least three times each employee's salary in your MSP – and a lot more if you're offshoring or outsourcing. The Vittoria Coffee family business was struggling when Les took it over. Instead of working the menial jobs, he focused his efforts on marketing and growth, with outstanding success.

## Ramping it up

When we opened our offshore office we decided to ramp it up:

- Instead of having one person answering the phone, let's have three.
- Instead of having one technician with that skill, let's get five.

And we quickly built that scale, giving us an enormous competitive advantage.

Smaller MSPs really struggle to do that, and they end up in the leaky bucket situation with customers seeping out and not being replaced quickly enough.

Here's another mini-drama – a customer rings up demanding fast service (a squeaky wheel gets the grease). You don't want to lose that customer, she jumps the queue, and you start servicing that customer really well. But what about the others? Their service level has undeservedly dropped, and they're jumping around complaining. Eventually at least one of them falls out of the bucket.

The problem facing these businesses is they don't have enough scale, and those enterprises are going to be constantly stifled through customer dissatisfaction because they will never get beyond a certain barrier, which tends to be somewhere between $500,000 and $1 million in annual revenue. They never get through the barrier because of the leaky bucket syndrome.

## The leaky bucket syndrome

Why do you have a leaky bucket? The two most common reasons are:

- you're losing customers
- you have hidden costs.

We've discussed losing customers, and there are quite a few hidden costs when you actually look at the revenue figures: generally speaking, up to 50% comes from computers, software and equipment that you're selling (at a low margin), and the rest is labor. So the true value of your business is really your staffers billing for their time. The margin is all in the labor.

MSP businesses may think they're product-based not labor-based businesses – but they've got all these staff members! Either the staff is doing the work or it's you that's doing it. Even though you might sell some product, some computers, some software, and even though you might have automated how to fix some of the problems, at the end of the day you still have staff.

People argue, 'No, it's all automated James – we use an RMM (remote monitoring and management software), we have awesome workflows in our helpdesk software, it's not labor intensive'.

Then why have you got employees?

Answer: because managed services is still a labor business.

### The true cost of labor

The true cost of labor is a hidden cost. The market average of wages in an MSP is $65,000 pa at the time of writing. That appears to only be $35 per hour that is paid to the employee while the business charges $150 to $180 per hour. So that employee seems cheap – but here's the hidden cost: the employee doesn't work 52 weeks a year, 24 hours a day. Furthermore, they don't work every day (and every night) of the week, they don't work weekends, and they certainly don't work 365 days a year. Where I'm from, in Australia, they have four weeks of annual leave (a couple of weeks in the US), but people take sick days too, they come in late, and they take holidays.

Worse – employees do not bill all of their time to customers. When we examine the numbers, we learn employees give away a lot of their time on the owners' behalf. For example, one MSP has a policy that if it's just a five-minute job for a regular customer – perhaps someone who has purchased hardware from them – they do it free. They can't actually bill for those five minutes. Doing so would seem petty and that would unsettle customers. In most cases employees bury such time in fixed-fee managed service contracts.

The market industry average shows that around 60% of employee time is billable. So the true hourly rate of your employee is in fact two to three times what you think you're paying them. If they are a $100,000-per-year employee, by the time you factor in all the downtime, it doesn't scale.

> We now live in the global economy, and offshore countries with a mature labor market can dramatically reduce your staffing costs.

What happens is that even though 'John' is only operating at 65% capacity, he's too busy on a job to handle anything else. Another group of jobs pops up, so you think, 'I'd better hire another John'. So you hire Matthew. But he's only operating at 60% capacity, and he can't be in two places at once either, so you hire a third person. You've now got John, Matthew and Amelia, and that's quite a wage bill. By adding more people you're actually creating a financial burden on the business. You are not recouping the value of those employees because they cannot work back-to-back, job-to-job, job-to-job, job-to-job. That's the hidden cost of an MSP.

Labor costs are actually the main point of this book, because the cost of labor is constantly going up. We now live in the global economy, and offshore countries with a mature labor

## Why so many MSPs are spinning their wheels

If someone rings you up and says, 'It's only going to take five minutes, would you mind taking a look at it?', your employee is charging you but not charging the customer. That doesn't fit into our business model at all, and it shouldn't fit into yours. We're not talking about a local regular customer popping into their local coffee shop now and then and having a chat with the owner, we're talking about 15 minutes in every hour that they might be writing off. That's why so many MSPs are spinning their wheels and struggling.

MSPs with small business clients find it's good customer service to spend 15 minutes and not bill them for it. But those MSP businesses may have 50 people phoning up and saying, 'I just need some advice, my wife's laptop is playing up, she's got some great photos on it – could you just help me out for 15 minutes?' Next someone else can't send an email. Another customer has forgotten her password and can't log in. Each one is a small problem. Fifteen minutes here, 10 there – add them up and it's a big problem. You may find you or your staff have just worked a couple of hours for free. And you don't want to keep hiring staff who are consistently giving away their labor.

You might walk into your local accountant and say, 'I've got a very quick tax question'. He'll say, 'Of course, I'll answer your quick question…'. That's good business for them. They are a small, local, friendly provider – they look after you. That's part of the success of their business. And accountants often charge much more than MSPs, and so are usually not looking to scale in the same way. And customers are probably happy to pay a little more in fees because they have a reciprocal relationship, they're a local business, and they see each other in the street.

But you can't just walk into KPMG or Ernst & Young or Deloitte and say, 'Can I just ask a quick tax question for no charge? I only need five minutes of one of your senior adviser's time'. It's a different dynamic. These accountants don't have that luxury; they're selling services, they've got to be sharp, they've got to be effective, they've got to charge for their time.

You need to value your time and your employees' time because you should all be well paid for what you do.

## Only paying for what you use

Here's one solution: when you outsource, you should only pay for what you use. So if my company steps in to do a job, we only do that one job. If you don't send us another job straight away we'll go and work on another customer's environment, and as far as our customer costs are concerned, we are on the job 100% of the time, 365 days of the year, 24 hours a day, but as our business partner you would only pay a fraction of that. You do not pay a full 100% of the salary as you would with an employee; you only pay for what you use. That's our business model at Benchmark 365.

We find most MSPs believe their 'effective' rate is $150 per hour. Just stop and look at that effective rate – it's more like $80! Most MSPs are too frightened to talk to their customers about the fact that they spent 50 hours working on their business that they don't bill and which they write off or bury in a fixed-fee agreement. Then when you factor in those other costs about staff not billing for their time, they're barely breaking even.

I think it's great looking after your customer, but I don't think it's great if you go broke doing it. I don't want to labor the point but I believe that if a company is utilizing my MSP's services for 15 minutes, say, 20 times a month, I'm absolutely going to charge them one way or another. I'm going to either put my hourly rates up, increase my fixed monthly fee, or I'm going to keep track of it until enough '15 minutes' have accumulated to a significant figure, and at a certain juncture I'll say, 'Here's the total'.

I let my customers know that as a professional service provider we always record our time and report to them on what we're using. That way they don't get 'bill shock', but it's incredible how many stop abusing the service when they realize that our time isn't free.

I've observed among MSPs at the conferences I attend that everyone likes to talk a big game. So despite the fact that their small IT business is struggling, when I ask them, 'How's business?', the person will invariably reply, 'Great, I've got a new customer', or, 'I've just bought this great new tool that's going to transform the business…'. I've asked that question and got that response, but when I look at their numbers, as I have done as an adviser, I frequently notice their business is barely staying above water. Realistically, if you're not growing you're declining – am I right? You know I am.

If you want to stay strong in business, watch the hidden costs and keep filling your leaky bucket.

## Questions to ask yourself

### *How committed to sales are you?*

Think back over the last two to three weeks. How much time did you spend actively seeking new business? This includes networking, marketing, straight-up sales calls, or even just thinking about how and where you are looking to source new business. Are you spending more than 80% of your time on sales?

### *How leaky is your bucket?*

What is your customer churn like? Are you adding more new customers than you are losing? On average, how long have your customers been with you? Go down your list and make an honest assessment of how happy you think each one is. Are they advocates of yours? Are they neutral? Are they constantly complaining? And for each – when was the last time you sat down and talked to them about their business? Finally, rank them as Advocate, Secure, Neutral, Unhappy or Out the Door. Obviously you want more towards the Advocate end than the Out the Door end.

### *How efficient and scalable is your business?*

What is your current percentage of utilized billable hours? Then work out your true effective rate per hour. Based on this rate and your utilized billable hours, if you want to scale, how many more staff will you need and what will it actually cost to do so?

# 4. HOW SCALING UP HELPS YOU LAND THE BIG DEALS

Scale enables you to step up as a trusted adviser – out of the server room and into the board room.

## Why scaling is important

In order to be competitive in today's environment, a one-person band doesn't cut it any more. It's no longer acceptable to say, 'I'll get back to you tomorrow'. Your customers are highly demanding and they want it done *now*. If you're too small, you don't have enough staff and you haven't got the strategy to extend your reach, you won't be able to get to your customers quickly enough.

Customers want more and more for less and less. Unless you have the resources to deal with that, chances are you're not going to be as successful as your rival businesses because you're not going to move quickly enough. That's why scale is important. It means having a more extensive sphere of influence, enabling you to service a bigger and broader customer base.

The other reason scale is important is it spreads the tasks, and in so doing it gives you back your life. When you're the only person doing the work there's always more left to do. Plus it's always urgent – you've got to do it *now*. You really can't pause to look at the big picture because you're dealing with all these distractions and emergencies. Scale lets you comfortably handle irritating phone calls like, 'Can you come around and fix this IT problem for me right now?'

Well no, actually – you'd rather:

a) take care of the emergency you're already working on, or

b) spend time with your family, or

c) get a bite to eat!

If you have a system in place to cope with overloads, you can relax about other people's emergencies and stay in control. You want to be free enough to engage other projects that help expand your business. You want to enjoy your business success – given that on the surface $1 million is a pretty decent turnover for a small operation. But if you're stuck working in the business because you don't have enough people to answer the phone and fix the IT problems, you've left yourself no room to move. You're on the tools. You're in the business. You're dealing with the chaos.

## 4. How scaling up helps you land the big deals

Scale enables you to step into your role as the expert adviser and not spend the bulk of your working time playing the role of firefighter.

MSPs usually take care of businesses that have 10, 15, 20, 50, 100 computers. Bigger MSP businesses may have a raft of irritated callers phoning up at the same time. Someone can't send an email, another can't log in, someone else can't download Adobe Flash Player. That's 15 minutes here and 10 there. Add them up and you'll see that your staff has just worked a couple of hours for free.

> If you have a system in place to cope with overloads, you can relax about other people's emergencies and stay in control.

The bigger operators tend to be in major cities, although there are some big regional businesses too. But a lot of small MSPs are happy to remain in regional areas, and there's nothing wrong with that. Those owner-operators may be happy running a smaller-scale business.

There must be more than one million businesses in Sydney, Australia (where Benchmark 365 began), and of those, a lot tend to be bigger and need to outsource their IT labor to ensure it's running effectively. Their providers aren't little computer shops; these MSPs play in a bigger commercial arena. They don't deal with residential. They deal with medium-to-big businesses, and their primary model is to go out and sell 12-month, 2-year or 3-year contracts to maintain the business's IT systems. Some of these operators have government contracts. These businesses are frequently struggling. I say, 'Instead of hiring more and more staff, outsource the key functions of your business – like answering telephones, resetting passwords, scanning for viruses, everything that happens day to day in a business – while you focus on marketing and sales. Go out and grow the show. That's *your* job.'

## Landing the big deals

When you're a one-person, two-person, three-person MSP business, the most dreaded question you ever get asked by a good-sized potential client is, 'How big are you?' If you can get out of that question and look good, you may enjoy a great opportunity.

Say you've got a meeting with Madeline, the director of a fast-growing medium-sized operation. You're psyching up: *this is going to be great … I'm going in for a meeting. I'm going to nail it.* Madeline says, 'Tell me a bit about your business…', and you answer with confidence. She asks about your team's expertise, and you're comfortable with that. Then she says, 'How big are you? How many staff have you got?'

And you stretch the truth a little…

If you've got three you might say six.

If you've got six you might say 12.

If you've got 12 you might say 20.

## 4. How scaling up helps you land the big deals

It's the most dreaded question because you're sure you can service Madeline's business, but if you answer truthfully she will probably think you're too small.

And you're a bit worried, too. What if she gives you more work than you can comfortably handle?

That's where scale comes into play, because if you're using an outsourced provider you can answer that question with confidence and say, 'Actually, we can handle anything you care to throw at us!'

Instead of waiting 15 years to get to 50 people like I did, with outsourcing you can say, 'Yes Madeline, we can handle it. We're ready, we're 24 hours a day. Call us any time, our expertise covers all your requirements.' And Madeline signs the contract.

Because of this lack of confidence, smaller operators are missing out on bigger opportunities because buyers are saying, 'You may be too small for us; we're worried you're not going to be able to scale up when we've got a big problem.'

Benchmark 365 – my company – solves that problem for you, and in so doing we give confidence to smaller operators. We act as them, so they can walk out the door and sell…

>    and sell…

>        and sell…

>            and grow.

They can suit up, face the client (whatever size they are) and say, 'I'm going to take care of it for you. Our team is ready to look after you now.' Numbers are no longer your problem.

We've got success stories of these MSPs who started out looking after businesses maybe the size of one small retail shop to now looking after large companies. After 12 months with Benchmark 365, they're picking up customers with an average of between 20 and 100 employees because they're confident and they now have the resources they need at their disposal.

## Scale up but maintain the relationships

In our line of business, things can sometimes get a bit heated. Imagine the client's system is down, they can't get onto the Internet, and they've got 20 people standing around idle. In situations like that, avoiding the customer isn't going to help. You need to press the flesh. You need to show genuine concern. You need to appease them. You need to go and see them and say, 'If only it wasn't our fault that it went down – but it is. I'm here now to help you get a result'. It's not perfect, but it sure beats avoidance caused by lack of confidence.

I like to find out in detail what my customer's business does. I try to find out even though sometimes I don't always understand it. I find out partly because I like to learn, partly for conversation, and mostly because it helps me service them better.

## 4. How scaling up helps you land the big deals

After they've explained what they do, I ask, 'Do you run any trade shows? Do you attend conferences or events?' And they say something like, 'Absolutely – we've got something coming up in April.' To which I say, 'Would you mind if I come and hear you speak?' My attendance has nothing to do with IT. It's to do with the relationship. Those customers – the ones for whom I show up at their speaking events (and the ones to whom I send birthday cards every year) – are the customers who spend the most money with our MSP by far.

Outsourcing will never be able to replace that local area marketing in our industry. Benchmark 365 can handle all the tech, but we'll never be able to press the flesh, send the birthday cards and be their friend. This is why you're the person who has the relationship with the customer and I'm the person who makes sure your business delivers first-class IT service 24/7, leaving you free to have those coffees and lunches with your client.

Never lose sight of the fact that this is a people business. It's all about relationships. Work out what your customer wants and how he likes to communicate. Older customers probably like to have a beer, Gen X probably likes sharing a light lunch, whereas even though the Millennial kids come in with the latest iPhones, iPads and iWidgets, and even though they're really tech savvy, they really don't want to do the fixing themselves because they're not running a computer business – they're running something else.

So despite them being pretty savvy with IT, the work is still there for you. They won't want to fix their own computers. They want to attend to whatever their business is supposed to be doing – theirs may be a digital marketing agency, a law firm, a small manufacturing plant or something else. So the sub-contract work is still on offer for the provider, and that's the truth of the matter.

> Never lose sight of the fact that this is a people business. It's all about relationships.

That's why you still need to go and see them and try to fit in with their way of communicating. Maybe you should upgrade to more modern technology. Because even though Millennials don't like picking up the phone, they still like to chat. No, they don't call each other much, and they probably don't want to phone you. They text or jump onto Slack or WhatsApp. But they have the same desire to communicate. The need is still there. Only the means of communication has changed.

### Why relationships are more important than ever

A company may want you look after their IT because you supply their hardware. They wouldn't haggle too much on the price, they just want you to look after it. You're the expert, remember? But times have changed. Smart business owners and especially Millennials now go online, check the price and buy online. Where you would once present the deal to the customer and say, 'We've spent hours figuring out the right laptop model for you…', what do the customers do now? They say, 'What's the model number?', and they get it much cheaper online. They use your advice – probably for free – and buy elsewhere.

Problem No. 2 is the margins on hardware have steadily declined as a result of online buyers. So when I use figures like $500,000 to $1 million, 30% to 50% of that could be made up of hardware. It used to be the cherry on the cake. It used to be a form of justification for other cash flow issues. 'Okay,' these MSPs would say, 'I admit I didn't do so well in that part of the business, but I just sold 10 new laptops and made quite a few thousand dollars out of that'.

Not so today – customers either don't buy the hardware off you at all, or they squeeze you down to 3% or 4% margin so that it's barely worth it. What looked like a healthy $1 million business is really a $500,000 business in decline. That's what's going on now.

### Becoming their trusted adviser

I have a conventional office but I spend a lot of time working out of lounges and coffee shops. This is now my life because I'm flying between countries. Sometimes I feel like a life coach. When you're in a service business you're also a therapist. I saw a client yesterday who's been with me almost the whole time I've been running my MSP. I don't have scheduled meetings with him, I just drop him a note saying, 'It's been a while, can we catch up?' He gives me a handshake, buys me coffee, sits down with me and talks about his business progress. My business is bigger than his now, so I advise wherever I can help. Plus, he sees me as his IT expert, so I answer everything he wants to throw at me about technology.

I never angle conversations towards computers. I ask general questions like, 'What's going on?' and let the customer lead. One client told me, 'James, what's going on for me is my business partner's just left and I've just found out there's a $400,000 debt that's got to be paid off and it's a big problem'. Based on that dynamic, I know that now is *not* the time to talk about upgrading his business's IT! Now's the time to talk and ask, 'What's that going to look like for you in the future Peter?'

'Grim, I guess.'

'Have you got a plan? Have you tried this? Have you tried that?'

He doesn't care whether I do the IT or not – if I empathize and help solve his other problems, he'll continue to buy from me for the next 10 years.

## Embracing the change

IT specialists are a professional group on the verge of being regulated once the government comes to terms with what's involved. They don't have a Code of Conduct, but countries are increasingly looking at ways to govern possible malpractice. The problem is it's such a fast-moving space

## 4. How scaling up helps you land the big deals

that the government's not on top of it. One thing we can say about change in this industry is, it's constant. It's very complicated and requires your best attention. Take it seriously.

What's the solution? MSPs are IT consultants first and foremost. You need to stop seeing the changes in the industry as threats, you need to embrace the new opportunities. Instead of trying to deter customers from taking a leap into new technology, MSPs need to help the customer make those decisions.

If a customer comes to me and says, 'We're looking at moving to product X in the Cloud – and you won't be supporting it', my response is, 'That's a fantastic idea … can I sit down with you and go through the decision-making process? I can manage this for you and I'll take an unbiased approach.' As a result, I build a lot of trust with the client, and that client usually keeps me on and continues to pay me the same amount of money because I've become their trusted adviser in my area of expertise. I gave them honest advice that was best for them.

The IT industry is still thriving today because you've got people like me who can explain it, take care of data, make sure everything is backed up, and who ensure no one can be malicious and delete data. Those sorts of reasons are a significant part of why the industry is thriving, because *you* understand it and the customer does not.

## Questions to ask yourself

*How would your business change if you could pursue larger deals knowing that you could quickly and easily scale up as needed?*

What keeps you up at night when it comes to the rapid pace of change in the MSP business? Now a bit of therapy. First, acknowledge it's scary. Then ask – what's the opportunity for you? And work out what you need to do to capitalize on it.

*Are you a supplier or a partner to your customers?*

Being a partner means you have a vested interest in helping your customers find solutions to problems, helping them to be more profitable and using your expertise to help them grow. Are you actively helping your customers weigh up the pros and cons of alternative technologies?

*What can you do to establish yourself as a trusted adviser?*

Are you an expert in IT or an expert in your customer's business? Understanding what makes your customer tick could lead you to far bigger opportunities. Are there any industry articles that might help your customer with a problem they're having? How about sending them a copy of an interesting book you've read? Does your customer run tradeshows or hold seminars? Do you attend and learn about them and their customers?

# 5. GETTING RHYTHM IN YOUR BUSINESS

> MSPs rely on the heroics of their employees to keep the business going.

## The difficulties of part-time staff

I believe you should outsource, and here's why. Cadence (rhythmic pattern) is one of the most crucial elements in creating a reliable business image, the ability to continue to move forward without distraction.

I'll give you an example. Her name was Irene, and she used to come into my office every Monday to do our bookkeeping. One day per week meant if I had a bookkeeping issue on a Tuesday I had to wait until the following Monday for Irene to fix it. I also had to wait up to six days to pay a bill, which didn't always suit my suppliers. We didn't have any rhythmic pattern in our bookkeeping. That's what I mean by the word 'cadence'.

Irene eventually retired, leaving me to ponder how to replace her. I eventually outsourced that aspect of my business to a bookkeeping company. They are a 24-hour-a-day bookkeeping company, and anything I wanted done was being immediately handled at any hour of any day. So we got cadence in our financials. As a result, our billing was faster and payments started being collected more quickly.

A major problem with part-time staff, compared to outsourcing, is that 'your day' might be Friday, not any other day. Even though it might be urgent, your part-timer doesn't want to talk to you on Tuesday because that's someone else's day.

You're a small business, you're trying to grow, you can't afford to hire from the top end of town, you can't afford $150,000 salaries. MSPs cannot afford to pay big salaries, so they hire from the lower end for maybe $40,000 and say, 'I'm gonna train you'. And they do.

On average, these $40,000 pa employees will spend one year with that business. They'll stay until a bigger company with deeper pockets comes along and hires the $40,000 person (now trained by you) for $80,000. That's the mistake I made. I hired staff any way that I could, and I'd tell them, 'I can't afford a big salary but I'll train you up'. The average tenure was 12 to 18 months, and then a big company would poach them. So I had to keep coming up with more recruitment costs and more training costs.

Staff turnover is high because the good staff leave the small MSPs and are drawn into the bigger companies.

It's embarrassing facing your clients when that happens. They ask, 'What happened to Natalia? She was great.'

'Oh, she's gone … we've now got Fred.'

'I don't like Fred, he doesn't know my system!'

And we've got to start all over again, this time with Fred. After a time everyone gets to love Fred, until Fred says, 'Sorry guys, I've just been given an $80,000 job offer'. The small MSP can't match it. So not only are these people billing only 50% to 60% of their time, they then leave and you've got to start over!

I used to get upset about that, but now I say to my young trainees, 'You just went from $40,000 a year to $80,000? Good for you.' And I'm still friends with many of them. But an MSP cannot sustain that level of upheaval. They can't afford to go around in ever-decreasing circles. Like a heartbeat, business needs to operate with a consistent rhythm. Obviously the anchor of this book is the staffing problem. That's why I started Benchmark 365.

It's a big problem that I needed to solve to feel stable.

## When you should insource

Why would I outsource rather than insource – say – my bookkeeping? I would outsource because that's not what I do best, it's what *they* do best. They keep up to date with the bookkeeping world so that I don't need to keep up to date with the bookkeeping world. I'm okay at bookkeeping, but I am not prepared to continually get myself up to speed. So I had to let that go.

I insource when I need to specialize in a particular area – so let's go back to my previous suggestions. There are some things that you *don't* want to outsource:

- **You don't want to outsource your relationship with your customer.** You want to be the person who goes out, sees them and talks to them. That's your relationship, and it's the basis of customer loyalty. You don't want to outsource that to a third party.

- **You don't want to outsource high-specialty skills that can only be found in your country or locality.** There are certain things that can be done well overseas, but there are other areas where the skillset is not there. So – when you're working out whether you should insource or outsource – itemize skills that are important for the growth of your business and evaluate what can be outsourced effectively. Consider the things that will give you cadence. And look at the things you must absolutely preserve to retain your competitive advantage.

As business owners, sometimes we can't stop ourselves from wearing too many hats. We build little empires in our businesses and start insisting we absolutely must be the one to do the books! We've got to be the one who answers the telephone! We must be the one who handles that customer's support ticket! Right? Yet we never consider doing our own legal work. We never think about doing our own plumbing. *We quite happily outsource certain things, and then we have an irrational issue with outsourcing others.*

> When you're working out whether you should insource or outsource, itemize skills that are important for the growth of your business and evaluate what can be outsourced effectively.

## Workers are being exploited ... in Western countries

People have suggested that outsourcing to places like India and the Philippines raises the issue of exploitation. But – I'm sorry to say – in Western countries we actually 'exploit' our own local workers. I regret the following example, but it's a real one and I don't think I'm the only person guilty of what I'm about to recount.

I had a talented employee who was our MSP's dispatcher. She was really good at her job, so I said, 'You're good at dispatch, so you might be good at invoicing and accounts receivable', and she was. So (in time), I added, 'And if you're good at the accounts, you might be good at...', and I thought of something else as well.

She was eventually on $60,000 pa, and my thinking was that because I was paying her so much money I wanted more and more value for my money. I was trying to shave my costs, and to achieve that I wanted to make sure she wore three or four hats in my business. So she ended up doing a bit of marketing, attending sales meetings with me, dispatching all the tickets, rounding up the technicians every day. Eventually she got to a point where she exploded with rage: 'I've got too many responsibilities!'

So when people suggest workers in the Philippines are exploited by Western businesses, I feel exactly the opposite and reply, 'I'm not speaking for all, but we certainly don't exploit anybody. I give them *one* job to do and they love it. They do it well, and they happily do it day in, day out.' I tell my staff, 'This is your pay' and 'this is your job'. I give them significantly above market pay, which is a very good middle-class wage. And all I expect from them is that they do their one job well. I don't ask for extra hours. I don't pressure them. That single task is all I expect from them every day, and they're happy and comfortable. You see, I've learned from my mistakes.

These countries have big international cities with big multinationals like IBM and Accenture and PwC, not to mention all of the major telecommunications companies having set up operations there. They've been there for the last 30 years. They have prestigious buildings like other business cities all over the world. Their employees get an education, work for these big companies, and get well trained. That's one of the things that has made a big impact on global business.

My employees have a car, some of them have the latest iPhone, a nice laptop, a great office to work in. They are neither impoverished nor exploited; they're being employed because they're good workers and they deserve to have a stable job. They put food on the table for their families every night, they live in a house or an apartment just like people in the Western world. Their lifestyle privileges are no different, just the economics are different. For example, in the Philippines, the cost of everything is about one-third of Australia, and one-quarter of the costs in America. You may find exceptions, but I can honestly say that I care about my team and I make sure they are being looked after properly.

But back home in Sydney, I see other business owners making the mistakes I used to make. I hear them say, 'Kimberley, would you mind working back a couple of hours tonight? Oh, don't ask me for overtime because you're already on this enormous salary.' That's what's happening in Western markets.

## Small business heroics

Small businesses rely on the heroics of their employees to keep the business going, as do MSPs. I hit that critical juncture when I was going to the Philippines for a break and I had that customer emergency. My technician was away sick and I *blamed* him! I exclaimed, 'He let me down!' But seriously, sooner or later each of your employees is going to get sick. They're not robots. They're going to have to take a day off eventually. That's why I wrote, 'Small businesses rely on the heroics of their employees'. Or else – what? All that's left is the heroics of the owner-operators – people like you and me. It falls to us to pull miracles out of our hats every single day!

That is asking too much of yourself, and of others.

When you outsource, you have a function you want done and that's all the contractors do day in and day out. If a customer has a problem, they phone us at Benchmark 365, where their call is handled by a professional, highly trained dispatcher. That person will triage the issue and the call will be transferred to a technician with that area of specialization. That's all they do, so they become experts in their field.

At Benchmark 365 we have a group of people dedicated to taking calls and dispatching. Their whole focus is to provide great customer service. That's all they have to do, and they have pride in doing it well. We also have another group of people dedicated to Level 1 support, and another group dedicated to Level 2 and Level 3. That's all those individuals do. They understand precisely what is required of them. They're confident because they can specialize in that particular competency. We've taken the uncertainty out of their job, while also providing training and a career path to progress to the next competency if they desire it. There is never any element of panic. As I said, they do it well – and they get to go home on time every day.

This contrasts with the average MSP whose numbers comprise – say – one owner and three staff. These owner-operators are running around doing a bit of everything. They do the hiring and firing, they oversee the books, they do sales and marketing, but mostly they still work as a tech. They haven't got the scale to drop that role. One minute they're working on a printer problem, the next it's a complex network for a bunch of hotels. They can't focus. If something goes wrong, it becomes their responsibility and they're working back late on a Saturday night.

*Confession:* I was a shocking employer. I would run employees into the ground. To retain them I had to pay them salaries of $60,000 to $100,000, and I'd drive them because I had no choice. On those wages, I couldn't afford to add another employee or I'd go broke, so that employee had to be a superhero for me. I was struggling to create a better business environment, and in 2012 a lightbulb switched on in my head. I took a hard look at myself and saw I wasn't cutting it. I had high staff turnover, I was relying on heroics, my business wasn't making any money anyway, and I had to change. So I changed my attitude and decided to ask my team to specialize in certain fields. I said, 'Your job is to do X. I want you to do it well and I want you to succeed at it.' And they did. Now we have a low staff turnover, and even when they leave they keep coming back.

## Outsourcing options

There are different outsourcing vehicles. Here are three key options:

1 **Freelancers.** You use the services of a freelancer who has the particular set of skills or credentials that suits your needs. You're sure to find one on the Internet.

2 **Business process outsourcing (BPO).** This is like a recruitment agency. They'll place someone in an overseas job for you.

3   **White-label service provider.** That's what we do at Benchmark 365. We provide the service, we do the job, and you take all the credit by having everything done under your direction and attaching your brand name to the work.

Let's check out each of these options.

## Freelancers

Of the three, hiring a freelancer is the least desirable option for an MSP. People often do freelancing to augment their already-existing income, or they have a very small window of availability because they have another responsibility, such as a newborn child in the house or a separate line of study. A freelancer might have another job somewhere else and do a bit of work for you in their spare time. Freelancers are not available 24 hours day, and can disappear at any moment.

Freelancing is not an attractive option for getting momentum, developing cadence and building trust with clients. It's too come-and-go for medium- to long-term relationships, but sometimes it is useful for short, well-defined tasks. Freelancers are useful for jobs with a predefined beginning, middle bit, and end. They are great when there's a defined parameter. If you like your freelancer, you may engage him or her for follow-up projects.

You can turn freelancers off and on as you feel like it. You can say, 'Sorry, we're done now', and that's that. But this cuts both ways. They can turn *you* off just as easily.

Another disadvantage is freelancers have some anonymity, so you don't necessarily even know where they are located. MSPs deal with a lot of sensitive company information, so a roving freelancer – answerable to no one – entering someone else's IT system on your behalf is not ideal.

> Freelancing is not an attractive option for getting momentum, developing cadence and building trust with clients.

### Business process outsourcing (BPO)

A BPO business is a company that helps you to locate staff offshore. They basically act like a labor recruitment service. A company goes to market and makes it known they require the services of an IT person. The BPO advertises, and says something like, 'We can get you staff @ $599pm'. They hire the people, payroll them, and their client businesses pay the BPO every month for the number of heads they've hired on their behalf.

The advantage is that BPOs look after all the local issues, they make sure the taxes are paid, the healthcare is looked after, etc. They are basically a managing agency paid by their clients. They effectively do the hiring and firing. That's a really common model, but there are downsides too:

- **Problem No. 1:** Although they do the hiring and firing, you have to do all the training and managing.
- **Problem No. 2:** All you've done is save some money on staff, you haven't solved the momentum problem.

You've got to manage them. And they still can't work 365 days per year; they still take sick days, they still take vacations, and you still run into problems with cadence.

- **Problem No. 3:** Because of those limitations, you spend a lot of time managing and you end up with a management overhead in your business. You might have five people in India but you're not there in the office with them. It's really hard to manage. You've still got to wonder, 'What are they doing today?' You give it your final blessing but you're not really there, you're dealing with it over Skype.

- **Problem No. 4:** All most BPOs want to do is fill as many seats as possible. It's their business model. They get paid for every seat you take up in their office. At the time of writing, it's about $700 a seat. They're working to get as many of those seats filled as possible, so they'll endorse an employee, and because you have no way of evaluating the person, you typically respond, 'If you say so, let's hire them'. And you're left to train them, figure out what they're doing all day, and then manage them. It's a really clunky business model.

In view of the above four points, you end up saying, 'I'd better get over there', so all of a sudden you're back and forth to another country. All of a sudden your costs are going up, management overheads are peaking, you're having the same problems of inconsistency as you did with regular employees, and you're having the same billable time problems.

And don't forget about Problem No. 5: BPOs have no concept of the uniqueness of MSPs. You talk to them and they still go 'what's that?'

'It's IT.'

'Okay, we'll get you some IT guys…'

'No…we don't want just *anybody*. It's more specific than that!'

If you follow this path, you're probably saving money, but not enough in my opinion to make it worth your while.

### White-label service providers

A white-label business provides you with a service or product that you label with your brand. Benchmark 365 is a white-label provider; I'm a 'ghostwriter' for MSPs – I do all the work for them, take none of the credit, and none of the glory. It's all done behind the scenes; that's white label.

> A white-label provider that specializes in MSPs trains and manages the staff, handles the hiring and firing, ensures the skills are kept up to date, and you never have to deal with management overheads.

In addition to that, you don't pay when you're not using the service. So rather than having an employee who sits there all day utilized or not, with our white-label approach you pay for what you use, therefore costs are substantially lower than any other model.

A white-label provider that specializes in MSPs trains and manages the staff, handles the hiring and firing, ensures the skills are kept up to date, and you never have to deal with management overheads. You don't need to handle HR issues, and you certainly don't need to get on a plane to sort out your staff problems. You've probably already worked with other white-label providers, such as white-labeled backup solutions or white-labeled Cloud host providers.

## Questions to ask yourself

### *What's your staff turnover?*

On average, how long do you retain staff for? Of those that do stay – why do you think they stay? Why do you think those that leave do so? What kind of boss are you? How much time per year do you spend retraining new staff or filling in gaps for those that have left?

### *What's not your expertise?*

Of all the functions in your business – not just customer service – what is not a core skill set? Can you outsource it? Will it save you time and money and improve the output? If so – then do it! Ask the same question of some of your core services – like managed IT support. Yes, you can do it – but can you do it better, cheaper and scale it the way a white-label provider could?

### *What kind of outsourcing suits your different needs?*

Of the functions you identified for outsourcing, what model fits best for your business? Freelancers, BPO or white label?

# 6. OUTSOURCING THE NOISE AND THE REPEATABLE STUFF

> Unless you find a way to be agile and cut your costs, someone will market to your customer base and undercut you.

**Every business, including** managed service providers, has a mixture of low-value and high-value tasks that – like it or not – must be carried out by you or your staff each and every day. A low-value task might be something as simple as a password reset, whereas a high-value task could be a very detailed network and security audit.

The frustrating thing about low-value tasks is that although the customer places little to no financial value on the task, they still demand it be performed professionally, and often at a moment's notice. That's the paradox you're facing – these low-value tasks are just noise to them and expensive for you! While wages continue to increase in Western job markets such as the United States, Canada, Australia and the United Kingdom, companies *aren't* paying more for IT support services than they were more than a decade ago.

That's one reason that small, medium and big managed service providers are likely to be attracted to outsourcing to white-label service businesses.

> Never outsource your status as trusted adviser.

## So what can you outsource?

Outsourcing, particularly offshore, has been happening since the mid '90s. You can outsource:

- dispatch and office administration
- first-, second- and third-level support
- software development
- quality assurance
- lead generation
- appointment setting
- social media campaigns
- bookkeeping
- accounting
- marketing

- graphic design
- written material
- everything in your business that can be performed primarily online.

But *never* outsource your status as trusted adviser.

### You've squeezed me!

People are demanding lower and lower costs. MSPs who used to charge $150 per user per month for support are now down to as low as $30 in some markets. Then customers come back and ask, 'Why are you using offshore staff?' I tell them, 'You've squeezed me – there's no way we can deliver a service and stay in business unless we go offshore or outsource!'

In a market where customers are demanding things be cheaper, you can't afford Margie doing dispatch on a $65,000 pa salary. I've done the numbers and it's just not feasible in our industry unless you radically increase prices. Even other service industries like bookkeepers have dropped from being a reasonably well paid and respected profession charging $60 an hour to now as little as $8 per hour of service. Customers are cutting all of their supplier costs to the bone, which means MSPs can't pay big wages to people answering the phones when they can outsource to the Philippines for a minimal per-hour cost. Whether you think it's right or not, you can't afford to do it in Western markets any more.

Generally speaking, this is what's going on in every service business in the modern world. Accountants used to be empires – the work is now heading offshore. And the accountants are saying, 'My customers are now doing their tax returns online! My business has vanished! I used to earn really great money doing this.' Unless you find a way to be agile and cut your costs, someone else is sure to market to your customer base and undercut you. You've got to be ready for that. There are two parts to this equation: the customer relationship, and getting your costs under control.

## International outsourcing has come a long way

In the 1990s, big telecommunication companies, and other large predominantly US companies, set up offshore operations. They did this because their consumers were driving down the prices of mobile phones and Internet services to a level with which they could no longer compete on the mainland.

So they went overseas and set up operations. In the '90s and early 2000s, the service was terrible because the call quality was poor and the processes were really bad. Customers hated it. But 20-plus years have passed and a lot has changed:

- **Telecommunications are significantly better** than they were almost 20 years ago, so that's the first thing that's changed: communication quality and efficiency. The old days are gone. Even some of the least developed countries now have fiber optics running right around the country, extending around the world. So the Internet and subsequent call quality have dramatically improved.

- **Two generations have gone through the learning system.** The service provided may have been of poor quality in the late '90s and early 2000s, but since then two generations have gone through the learning system. The knowledge and skill of people has vastly improved, along with their proficiency.

- **The companies have learned what doesn't work and solved it.** With over 20 years of experience, outsourcing is now a totally different ballgame. My team are typically university-educated – or at the very least, some other form of qualification – IT professionals who have had customer service training and English-speaking training, and they are very good at what they do. They are no less qualified than my Australian staff, or employees in your typical MSP in the US.

I'm not saying it's a perfect system.

But it's not perfect where you are either.

So let's not complain about slightly foreign accents!

## Customers now want an instant fix

Cash-struggling MSPs will always have support tickets slip through the cracks because they don't have enough people working around the clock to keep on top of everything. Gone are the days when the customer picked up the phone, called the IT company and said, 'Barry, my emails aren't working', and 'I'll get to it real soon' was considered a satisfactory response.

Now it happens like this: the phone rings, someone might grab it, and that someone might promise a technician on the job within an hour (or they may not!). But customers become disgruntled because they've been left waiting. MSPs are constantly struggling with this problem because 'soon' is no longer fast enough. Customers want their demands met *immediately*. Given that everything in the world is now moving so fast, customers want their problems fixed as quickly as possible. They don't care *who* does the fixing, they just want it fixed so they can meet their targets and go home on time. If you can meet that demand, the customer could not care less who answers the phone or who does the job. Once their problem is solved, there is nothing to worry about.

We regularly survey our customers, and the conversation often goes something like this:

> 'Hi Mary – you had a problem with your printer a week ago…?'
>
> 'Yes.'
>
> 'You spoke with John Ramos. How was your experience?'
>
> 'I don't remember speaking to him.'

She doesn't remember! And that's a common response because it was over and done with in under two minutes.

If Mary had been made to wait she would have absolutely remembered. *You betcha!* If she'd had to wait a day for someone 'to get back to her', she would not forget that she had to wait all day.

### Your customer just wants speed and competency

Owners are not necessarily aware of technical IT problems. The business owner (your client) is busy doing what owners do (running a business). If she's got a problem with a computer the owner turns to her personal assistant and says, 'Can you call up the IT company and get the thing working again'. The owner delegates everything. She doesn't care about – nor necessarily understand – the processes that cause a computer breakdown, nor the process that gets them fixed. The Millennials may change all that, but at the moment there are millions of owner-operators who are uninterested, thinking about other things, and probably not computer savvy – and that's your client.

> Remember, you are the expert in an area that governs a whole chunk of your customers' business.

Your relationship with her is the key. It's not about the country she's in. It's about speed and competency to do the job well. It's also about your personal contact – or 'helping' – your client.

Some MSPs are reluctant to outsource.

'Why?' I ask, having shown them the processes that will grow their business.

'Because I'm worried what my customers will think…' is the reply.

That implies a misconception that customers will feel disconnected from you and your people. However, they actually have no reason to feel 'connected' during the fix-it side of your relationship. If anything, outsourcing the technical side gives you more – much more – time to connect with customers. You can talk about their families and their aspirations, and give them IT and business advice.

Remember, you are the expert in an area that governs a whole chunk of your customers' business. Whether they are in accountancy, manufacturing, renovations or retail, you are still the expert – not in the area of their core business, of course not – but there's a whole IT side you know about, and the accountant, manufacturer, renovator or retailer is counting on you to fill that need and help their business grow.

## Tracking your progress

We instantly send out a survey after every ticket we handle. Say a customer calls us up because the office printer's not working:

1   We remote in and fix it.

## 6. Outsourcing the noise and the repeatable stuff

2   After we've fixed it, that caller will receive a ticket update asking, 'What did you think of our service today?'

We keep tabs on our satisfaction rating. As I write, our CSAT Score (customer satisfaction score) stands at around 94%. We're proud of this aspect of our business – we present it to potential clients and say, 'We've got a 94% satisfaction rating!'

Options for outsourcing and choosing the right partner are one and the same. So choose the right partner, one that understands your business. Find a partner that understands the key drivers for your business to succeed.

So you've implemented some outsourcing in your business. You've reduced your costs, you're under control, everything's humming along, and it's going great – now what? Get skilled up, surround yourself with a sales mindset not a tech mindset, and get into the habit of going out and filling up that leaky bucket.

## Questions to ask yourself

### *Are you a tech or an entrepreneur?*

How do you think of yourself – are you a tech or an entrepreneur? You can only grow your business if you think of yourself as the latter.

### *What do your customers think about your service?*

Have you surveyed your customers? What do they think of the service you provide? Ask them what's most important: getting something fixed ASAP, or talking with the same locally based technician every time – even if they have to wait?

### *What are your assumptions?*

What do you assume to be true about outsourcing and offshoring? When was the last time you had an experience of offshoring? Speak to your peers who use it in their business – what do they think of it? You can read our case studies here: www.benchmark365.com.

# 7. TAKING TOTAL CONTROL OF YOUR DAY

> Imagine not being on the tools.
> Imagine being in total control of your day.

## Imagine that

By 2014 after successfully scaling my MSP, I was running it overlooking a beach. I saw myself pulling out my iPhone and checking that all the formal work had been done in my business, checking everything was moving through the system, and new sales leads were coming in. Like the end of a satisfying movie, I slipped my phone back in my pocket and wandered off into the sunset.

My life wasn't always that pleasant. I used to roll over in bed, check my phone in the morning and go, 'Oh damn! Clare's server's down and Justin's not coming into work today – damn it!' Next question: 'What else have I got to urgently deal with?' That's what most MSP owner-operators are going through right now. MSP owner-operators are certainly overworked. It's hard for these people. They're stuck in a cycle. Not only are they working long hours but the rewards aren't there when they're done.

> When you scale your business to insource or outsource enough support staff you can actually focus on the things that are important.

The standout problem is the high cost of labor. Time means money. When you work out how to leverage labor costs against the things I've told you about in this book you will get profit, growth and the occasional day off. Imagine waking up in a more relaxed state. Imagine not being on the tools. Imagine being in charge of your day. Imagine working on the pursuits that are best for you, your business, your family and your life. Imagine starting each day not having to log in to your helpdesk software to check how many support tickets have been raised. Imagine driving to a client's premises, catching up with him, and talking about how you can service his business to greater advantage. Imagine choosing how you'll do your day, every day, instead of being distracted by customer demands.

Imagine that.

When you scale your business to insource or outsource enough support staff you can actually focus on the things that are important, and you also get to spend more time on what you have really set out to achieve.

## Giving your customers something to talk about

Customers buy from people that they trust, so you must put time into your customers. The challenge is, how do you get as much face time with a client as you possibly can? How do you add value to their business? How do you bring something new and exciting to the table?

Answer: outsource the repeatable stuff and outsource the noise and distractions, so you can gain control of your day. Then you can take your foot off the accelerator and relax with your customers. Warm them up. Make them like you. Keep them loyal. Make yourself memorable.

Here's a quaint idea: you want to give your customers something they can talk about – at home, at a BBQ, over a drink – right? Show them some cool new tech they won't have seen. That's not difficult for you because you work in the technology sector, a sector that's coming up with new innovations every week. So show them a cool app or bring the latest wearable tech along and say, 'Have you seen this? It checks your heart rate, it does this, does that…'. That's how I sometimes amuse my customers. They smile when they see me coming, and say, 'What have you got now?' And I show them something new, something they can talk about after I've gone.

Tell your customer something they haven't heard before and they'll share it with somebody else because it makes them sound good. All you're doing is winning their interest. They'll brag about it to other people, and you'll come up in their conversations: 'My IT guy's got this amazing interactive whiteboard that transcribes your meeting notes and lets you jump into a call with another country and translates the call into another language in real time.' It's social currency. It's also a passive form of advertising that reinforces your expertise.

After a while, they'll expect something from you when you turn up. They'll ask, 'What new gimmick have you got now?' They'll enjoy talking about it, and that indirectly places the conversation right in your line of business. It's like selling without the sales pitch. After all, you're not 'selling' and you're not closing. You won't have to.

## You're a leader, not a tech

One problem MSPs and small business management face is they cease doing the very things to which they owe their success and they upskill into management. Suppose you can make the best pen ever made, and suppose you become successful because of this wondrous pen – you then stop making the pen and start running a pen-making office. That's the folly the small MSP owner has to face. Because they're great at fixing computers, they end up in management and they need to make a radical about-face in their skillset. If you're a small MSP owner, that's probably where you're at right now.

All these problems you never had as a tech come up – you've lost control of your working life, Donna hasn't shown up for work today, John's forgotten to phone back a client, you've got to call on a client to get paid, you're trying to do too many things at the same time, and you haven't got a strategy in place to handle the pace of change.

> One problem MSPs and small business management face is they cease doing the very things to which they owe their success and they upskill into management.

This was my story too. I stretched my working life beyond reasonable bounds and exhausted myself. Then I started to think outside the box and do things differently from the rest of our industry. I started to research things that would be of value to my customers. Only then did I start to see some blue sky, and that led to the growth of my business.

The second thing I was able to do with my customers was talk more about their stuff and less about IT. Customers want you to *fix* and *maintain* their systems but they certainly don't want to sit around talking about it. They want to talk about their teams' performance. They want to talk about some new tech they've just bought. They want to brag a bit about their latest and greatest achievement. Having explained their immediate dilemma, they want to move on and talk about anything other than the mechanics of their problems. They'd rather talk about the weather!

### Retooling yourself and your business

Because you're outsourcing, everything else is taken care of. You've got the cadence and the momentum and you're up and running. You now need to focus your energy and time on your next level of business.

After MSPs have outsourced the functional aspects of their business, they sometimes wonder, 'We don't know what to do – we no longer need to answer our phones, we're not handling all the tickets, we're looking at a blank screen trying to figure out what to do next…?'

Answer: work on business growth.

They ask, 'How?'

They are no longer on the tools, no longer doing tech support, no longer fighting fires. Therefore they have time to realign their thinking to their new concept of doing business, to become proactive, to skill up and to get good at sales (and there's a whole bunch of ways to do that).

I had to retool myself too. I did it by changing my habits. I now have time to promote my business and take care of managing. Instead of worrying about customer problems, every time I went for a drive I would listen to a sales podcast in the car, because I needed to learn about sales and the psychology of selling. When I'm not listening to podcasts about sales, I read books about sales. And when I'm not reading books about sales I go to seminars about sales.

I kept doing that over and over and over again until I finally realized, *hey, I'm actually getting really good at that – as good as I used to be as a tech*. And being good at something gives you energy in that direction. So retooling yourself can work for you as it did for me. I got good at things I never thought I'd be good at. First I gained knowledge, then I gained confidence. I now feel comfortable speaking to a roomful of people at IT conferences, and I never, ever, ever thought I'd reach that point. I was the little kid – remember – with the screwdriver, removing the back of my parents' shiny new PC and peering inside wondering what made it work. I'd never have dreamed I'd eventually run a business that fixed complicated IT problems for major companies! But I learned, the same way that you can too.

What you focus on expands.

'Aw…', you say, 'I don't know if I want to do that, James. I don't know if I'm very good at sales.'

I reply, 'Of course you're not very good at sales – you haven't been doing it! You've had your head stuck in the IT world for how many years? So it's time to learn and time to go out and grow your business!'

(I've read some great books, and I'm happy to share a list of recommendations. For a list of books that have really helped me, check it out online: visit www.benchmark365.com.)

### You have the capacity to reach millions

My favorite book on sales is called *How to Sell Anything to Anybody* by Joe Girard. I love the essence of that book, and I try to translate that into what we do in sales.

Joe sold 13,001 cars between 1963 and 1978, and was recognized by *The Guinness Book of World Records* as the seller of the most cars in the United States in 1973. He was a master networker: everywhere he went he knew people, he knew their kids' names, he knew their anniversaries, he knew their birthdays, he knew when they last bought a car, and he would constantly pepper them with happy birthdays and 'congratulations on your anniversary'. He had a Rolodex (desk business card index) of everyone in town, and built up an empire of car sales.

Joe Girard sold thousands and thousands of cars, and everybody loved him because of his 'nice guy' tactics.

This was pre-Internet, but the exact same rules still apply, except now with the power of social media, email, and access to low-cost lead-generation services, you can be reaching out to people digitally. You can have tools reminding you to say Congratulations, Happy Birthday and Merry Christmas, whereas poor old Joe had to carry it all in his head. He was only able to hit a few thousand people.

You have the capacity to reach millions if you do it right.

## Getting help

Now that you're ready for growth, now that you've got your service delivery under control, now that you've got your business organized, now that you have the time to focus on growing the business, get out there and sell your services. Some of the tactics I've mentioned are a great starting point.

Selling can be a bit of a challenge. We can solve their cost problems, we can give them all these tools, we can say 'here it is, turn the key', but after that they might still struggle with

## 7. Taking total control of your day

'how do we sell?' So at Benchmark 365 we help them with sales too. We have the expertise and experience. Through out Peer Groups we point our partners in the right direction and provide modern tactics to help them sell more. Sales is a subject area all of its own, a different book. But I want to emphasize that we are mindful of this and we work with MSPs in this area. Work out what help *you* need, and make sure you find people who can provide that help.

And here's a suggestion: stop only going to the conferences that all the other MSPs attend. Start going to conferences that present new ideas on how to solve problems. You need to be agile. Instead of going to an MSP conference, go to a marketing conference. Or go to a sales conference. Learn about new business practices and different problem-solving options. And as a trusted adviser, as you're sitting down with your customer, you will have something new and exciting to share. You'll be telling them something that the other IT providers aren't telling them – that's the key.

> Work out what help you need, and make sure you find people who can provide that help.

Everything I've said about how to get skilled up, remembering your customers, celebrating the special events in their lives, that's exactly what I tell all our Benchmark 365 clients. We're not just an outsourced IT helpdesk, our sole mission is to help MSPs scale and be profitable. The way to do that is to get their service delivery under control and help them sell more effectively.

## Questions to ask yourself

### *What's your super power?*

Think about what it is your customers will most value from you once you outsource. What do they need in order for you to become a trusted adviser? What can you offer them that they can talk about?

### *How can you fill your sales and marketing gap?*

What conferences and events can you attend or local groups can you join that will help you build up the sales and marketing skills (or other business skills) you need to grow your business?

### *How can you retool your day?*

Make a list of every work-related thing you do in a week. What can you stop doing and replace with new habits or activities that will help upskill you where you need it? What tasks can you introduce into your day targeted at growth and building better customer relationships?

# 8. THE BENCHMARK 365 WAY

> In an industry estimated to be worth USD$960bn per year there is no need to stay small. There is no need to stand still.

**Having read my book,** the first thing you must do is: *get your business under control.* It's a message I keep re-emphasizing. We started the early chapters with a list of challenges and opportunities. Then we solved them by introducing the concept of outsourcing. You don't have to be great at tech support to be an expert on technology, all you need to do is connect the dots for your customers and get a trained expert to do the leg work. 'I'll get one of my engineers to give you a call and explain everything in detail,' is all you need to say. I suggest you outsource the tech mindset aspects of your MSP and concentrate on the customer relationship and the selling.

This is at the core of what I like to call the Benchmark 365 Way. These are the key tenets:

- The ultimate goal is business growth – the number one focus of the MSP owner is customer relationships and selling.

- Outsource to increase the services and expertise you provide your customers.

- Outsource to drive down costs and give you on-demand scale.

- Constantly benchmark (measure) your business metrics against comparable businesses, to signpost areas that need further attention.

- Outpace your competition not by putting a line that says '24×7' support on your website but by backing up that claim with an entire team available to your customers day and night.

- Learn from your peers – there's enough opportunity for everyone, and there's nothing like engaging with your community to help you solve problems and capitalize on opportunities.

The key is to make your business grow *and* to grow your profits.

Once you have this new mindset, it's time to zero in on a few basics to make sure your new business strategy is set up for success.

Let's have a look …

## Fix the inconsistencies

Having decided on your new business strategy, the first thing you should do is fix your inconsistencies. For example, one day all the team members are there – Adam's here, Joni's here, you're here, phones are ringing, support tickets are getting solved. Next day Adam's away sick, Joni's on vacation, customers are calling, customers are screaming.

So get some cadence into your business. Get it running smoothly. Outsourcing will certainly help, but it's not the total picture. Back in your office you have staff to organize with new and exciting opportunities, but you have to manage them nonetheless.

## Get a mirror that works

How do you know which areas require your attention? Answer: get a mirror that works. Take a good hard look at your financials. I do it by routinely checking my financial dashboard and asking myself, *where is the bucket leaking? Where am I losing money?* Is it an 80/20 answer? (Roughly 80% of the effect comes from 20% of the causes.) I reevaluate my costs and take a good hard look at the true profitability of my customers.

Instead of thinking, *I like Sarah, even though I'm not really sure if I'm making money off her…*, I say, *hang on, there's something not right here…!* So we separate products/hardware/software revenue from our services income. The conclusions become self-evident. The results will tell you which customers are profitable and those that are not. I suspect not all your clients are as profitable as you might think they are.

And not all of your staffers are as busy as they tell you they are. It's harsh but true. I've seen it. Having measured your customers, look at your staff. Ask – which staff members are billable and which staff members are not?

> **How do you know which areas require your attention?**
> **Answer: get a mirror that works.**

Having seen the reality of where you're losing money, I'm not suggesting you then go out dumping customers and sacking staff. I don't want to say 'get rid of people' – I want you to see the delivery gaps. Knowing what's going on is a form of control. How you handle it is up to you. Are the phone lines always available to your customers? If 'yes', does this mean you're taking phone calls at 10.00 pm? Or does it mean that some days your customers get good service and some days they get poor service?

One of our Benchmark 365 partners called me and said, 'I'm in a lot of trouble, I have to let three of my employees go.'

I replied, 'Maybe you do or maybe you don't. I'll give you a hand checking that out. I'll help you get some of the work done, help you free up some cash flow.'

He didn't actually need to sack anybody because he busied himself with getting more clients – and he's doing really well now. He's from Melbourne, Australia, and he recently told me proudly, 'I've just picked up a client in Sydney'. He's stretching his wings. He's finally out of the trenches. That's the level of freedom you can have.

## Fill those delivery gaps

Now you've identified your delivery gaps, fill them through outsourcing.

MSPs that outsource to the right partner don't have to worry about sick days, vacations and tardiness, or stress about too many IT issues occurring at once and overwhelming you and your helpdesk. MSP owners no longer need to fill in for their absent employees or perform miracles when customers demand more than you can handle. A good outsourcer fills in all of those gaps, ensuring your business has capacity and maintains the momentum for you.

And why is this momentum so important? Because instead of you stepping in to provide tech support to your clients, you're stepping *up* into marketing and sales to grow your business.

Something that I never realized would happen as a side effect of scaling up my MSP is that the more time I spent selling, the more attractive our products and services became. All that extra time I gained from getting off the tools and spent talking to clients about business problems meant that I could appreciate their needs better and start to get more insight into what my customers wanted. That's what made us a market-leading MSP, and it can absolutely be the same for you too.

## No borders

The paradigm has changed: business is now borderless. Outsourcing gives you the capacity, scale and time that you didn't have before. So think outside your locality. That leads to interstate and even international possibilities.

Even though I had an office in the Philippines, I still wasn't thinking internationally until someone came up to me and said, 'We're opening an office in Singapore – can you help?'

My instinctive response was, *no, we're a Sydney IT company* – then I realised, *no, we're not, we're actually a global IT company! If we can service all of our Australian customers from the Philippines then there's nothing stopping us servicing anyone's customers in any region.*

That was a big eye-opener for me. And I want you to start thinking, *do you really need to limit your operations to your immediate locality?* Broaden your horizons. If you're on the west coast, maybe there's a way to get a foothold on the east coast too. If you're in the north of your region, who is to say you can't take on the south?

Not everyone sees things as I did. A lot of people might say, 'Good for you if you want to take that risk and open up in five different countries, but we'd be just happy if we could pick up some business in the next town.' I also hear a lot of people saying things like, 'I've always limited myself to my local town, but I've always wondered if there were opportunities in the neighboring town. It's only 30 minutes away. Could we expand?'

Yes you can.

## The Benchmark 365 Way in action

Benchmark 365 is designed by an MSP to help other MSPs grow profitably. Our business is always adapting to industry change, but I'd like to step you through how the Benchmark 365 Way works in practice today.

> When customers are happy your business will grow.

### Step 1: Pulse check

I've always believed that what gets measured gets managed. A lot like weighing yourself before you start a new fitness program, we do a bit of a weigh in of sorts with our new Benchmark 365 partners too.

We want to measure, what is your customer experience like today? How long does it take to identify and solve a problem? Are you consistently delivering your services, or are there gaps to be filled?

Once we have a baseline, we start working toward a better result, or 'the benchmark'. This measuring and checking happens throughout our relationship, making sure we're always focused on delivering better customer experiences and profitable MSP performance.

### Step 2: Build the support engine

The core of our business is our helpdesk services. Most MSPs struggle to deliver a consistent, reliable service for their customers, and it's our goal to smooth this part of your business out so you can focus on selling and growing.

It starts with assigning you a team of competent and dedicated personnel, and learning everything there is to know about your processes and sharing our own expertise and experiences too. It could be that you have amazing documentation, or you might not. It doesn't matter. No MSP is perfect. We work together as a team to smooth out the kinks to give your clients the best possible support experience day and night. When customers are happy your business will grow.

### Step 3: Build your sales confidence

If you're like me and started your MSP because you were good at tech then you've spent a long time finding the answers to problems inside your computer. Perhaps every day until now you've logged in to your helpdesk system to find out what's happening with your customers' IT and to help them fix it.

All of that has to change. The answers to your customers' business problems are not on a screen on your desk. They're out there in the real world talking to real business owners with real business problems, and fixing those problems by finding and selling them a solution.

Through our peer groups and social media community we share best practices, resources, and almost two decades of sales experience to help you sharpen your expertise and grow your MSP revenue.

### Step 4: Benchmark your performance

The average Benchmark 365 partner doubles their revenue in the first 12 months (see our website at www.benchmark365.com for case studies and examples).

> Remember – what gets measured gets managed.

We believe that Benchmark 365 partners are the most profitable in the IT industry because they have significantly reduced labor cost, do larger and more profitable deals, and have much lower overheads than a traditional Managed Service Provider.

Often MSPs are struggling to get past a particular issue like pricing services – through benchmarking we identify these issues and work with you to solve them once and for all.

Remember – what gets measured gets managed.

## The first three months

The first three days working together are a big eye opener for our new partners. In fact, the first month can be a little confronting – that's why we call it a pilot. You can imagine – they've done the same thing day in, day out for a decade, and we come along and point out 'a better way'. We're confident because we know from experience. They're not so confident because everything is new.

The second month it gets better, and by the third month they disappear on vacation, and when they come back they no longer want to talk about tech support. All they can think about is how to maximize this new engine powering their business. Some MSPs have come to us saying, 'I hope you guys are ready because we're bringing in five more deals this month'. We say, 'sure'.

However, I do believe in careful partner selection. If it's not going to be a fit, it's bad energy and it won't work for us or them, so we're very selective. The arrangement is that Benchmark 365 is your partner, we're in business together, and I'm taking a risk on your business. We've got to be in sync with each other because:

- I'm expecting that you're going to go out and grow
- you're expecting that I'll deliver.

Our team are treated like partners as well because they've got a goal. We've all got goals:

- Yours is to grow your business.

- Mine is to grow your business.
- My team's goal is job satisfaction – they want our partners and your customers to be happy.

### We eliminate all inconsistencies

As an outsourcing option, we underpin everything other than the customer relationship. When the phone rings – we answer. When someone's got a problem – we fix it. But we can't replace their local area support. When people sign up with Benchmark 365, the first thing we do is help them through their delivery inconsistencies so there is no more disruption, no apparent sick days, no sudden exits. The business just runs smoothly, tickets are being resolved, the end user is happy, and it's all done professionally from the Philippines.

This is what I mean when we say we're a white-label company. We become the first point of contact. When the customer calls up with a problem, the phone is diverted to our team and we say, 'Hi, thanks for calling … ' – and we say the name of your company.

The customer says, 'I've got an IT problem…'.

Details pop up on the screen so that our operators immediately know the caller's history, and we say, 'Great to hear from you, we just want to confirm this is the right phone number to get you back on?'

'Sure.'

'How can we help you?'

'I've got a problem with our email.'

'No problem – we'll get that off to an engineer.'

Then we take the details, fix it and call back: 'Just letting you know, we've logged in and fixed your email problem.'

'Great.'

'Is there anything else we can do for you?'

'No, that's fine.'

'Okay – have a nice day.' Click.

But it doesn't end there. There's follow up and customer satisfaction surveys too.

> It's a collaboration to make sure your customers are getting the support and attention they deserve.

Every single ticket we complete for a partner is surveyed to ensure the customer is happy with the result. We don't stop there either; if we have an inkling the customer is unhappy, whether it's from direct feedback or the tone of an email or phone call, we go out of our way to talk to them and see what we can do, and we don't leave our partners in the dark. We let them know, 'Hey, I think you should go and speak to Mary – she needs some TLC from you and your team.' It's a collaboration to make sure your customers are getting the support and attention they deserve.

## 8. The Benchmark 365 Way

### Benchmarking

We benchmark our partners – that's where our name comes in. We check them against similar operations and tell them, 'That IT company in North Carolina makes five times as much profit as you, with the same number of customers and the same amount of work. We're going to show you how to fix that. We're going to make you even more successful because we don't want you to look at us like an expense, we want you to look at us like we're your partner. We're here to help you grow and be profitable. We're not talking about cuts, we're talking about boosts.'

Once you've signed with us we do all your mundane work. We use real-time business intelligence tools, and we point out, 'This is where you're losing money. We've analyzed your business and that customer calls constantly – how much are you charging them?'

'We're charging $300 per month.'

'Well, you're losing money on that one – so let's help you to turn that customer into a happy but profitable customer.'

The client says, 'It's only five minutes here, just five minutes there…'

And we'll say, 'Your employees are charging you $60,000 to $100,000 pa for that, and you're not charging your client because it's "only" five minutes!'

We confidentially show them MSP-A and MSP-B. Why have they got this and you've only got that? You're in the same business. You've got the same number of customers. You've got the same dynamics, products and services, but this business is there and yours is only here: 'It's you, it's *you*!'

'Is it?'

'It is. And I'll give you the skills and tools to get you up there as well!'

At Benchmark 365 we make it a policy to under-promise and over-deliver. We want to *wow* their clients, and they stick with us because we deliver and it's a win–win.

## How can you find out more about Benchmark 365?

Our website is the best place to find out more about us. We're www.benchmark365.com, and we regularly run webinars, and publish white papers and blog articles aimed entirely at helping MSPs grow.

Most small businesses don't talk to anybody else, they don't share their pain with anybody else. Once you're signed up with Benchmark 365, you join a virtual peer group so everybody's together in a forum where we share sales strategies, ways to improve, and ways to optimize your business and be more profitable.

And they love it.

They love it because they say, 'No one ever told me about this. I never saw the forest from the trees. I thought I was doing quite well!'

## 'Go to Europe – we will run your business.'

By 2016 my MSP was going really well, but something was missing for me. I wanted to help others in our industry accomplish the same thing but when I tried to show them the ropes it was really difficult for them. We were making it look easy to hire an offshore team, but I'd spent the better part of four years living in or travelling routinely back and forth to the Philippines. I wanted to help, but nobody wanted to spend years building what we had built.

One day an overwhelmed MSP-owner called Martin rang me up and said, 'I haven't had a holiday in six years. I've been at this for 10 years. I never see my family on weekends. We haven't been away. I want to take them to Europe. I don't think I'm doing it right.' Martin was an example of the small operator, overworked, not doing it right. Does that sound familiar?

I said: 'Go to Europe and our MSP will take care of your helpdesk.'

We took every one of Martin's phone calls and emails and ran his helpdesk, and his customers were genuinely thrilled to see Martin get some time away and to get a whole team of people working on their support tickets. We solved problems, and his customers got *better* service. We have more technical expertise because he could only do so much as a one-man show, so he might be good at one narrow part of IT but we've got a lot more team members which allows us to have people who specialize in different areas. At that time we had 50 people. There are experts on the team that can solve anything that comes our way.

He went to Europe, he never called me once, and he was more profitable during that trip than if he'd stayed home.

When he came back four weeks later he said, 'How do I keep this going?' – and that's how I started Benchmark 365.

I said, 'This works for you – I'm going to do this process again. Can you tell someone?'

He said, 'I've told everyone I know', and he's referred countless partners to us.

Today he's doing what I told him to and reaping the rewards. He listens to sales podcasts every day, attends sales seminars, reads books, and every time I talk to him he's got another customer,

> … got another customer,
>> … got another customer.

He once asked, 'I'm growing so fast, have you got the capacity to handle us?'

'Yes,' I replied, 'I'll go and hire more people – it's not your problem.'

We got another batch of people in, trained them up, got them ready, and said, 'You tell us when the customer's coming in and we'll get it sorted'.

## You got this!

There's a saying I really like: if you keep believing what you've been believing, then you'll keep achieving what you've been achieving.

In 2012 I believed I was doing all the right things to grow my MSP. I bought all the software tools the industry told me to buy in order to improve my business, and I attended all of the IT conferences to listen to experts tell me how to grow a bigger company, but something was bothering me – my business wasn't growing, and to be quite honest I wasn't really convinced that the experts were growing either.

I had to change my beliefs. I had to try a different approach, and I believe you do too if you want to succeed.

I believe all it takes is one foot after the other, applying the principles in this book to grow your MSP.

In a sector estimated by Gartner to be worth USD$960bn per year there is absolutely no reason to stay a small MSP, and there is no reason to struggle like I did.

My Eureka moment wasn't just a decision to travel to the Philippines. It was a decision to let go of my past beliefs about myself and my business and adopt new ones. It was a decision to live life surrounding myself with incredible people, to work with the best clients, to spend more time with my family, and to be happy.

If I can do it, so can you.

*To your success,*

*JV*

# CASE STUDY: INFINITE EDGE GETS INFINITE SCALE

Managing Director Martin Haak is the MSP I told you about earlier who needed some time away (in Europe) and helped bring Benchmark 365 to life. Here he shares more from his perspective on how outsourcing helped Infinite Edge grow dramatically in just one year.

Founded in 2010, Infinite Edge is an MSP based in Melbourne, Australia that specializes in the delivery of IT support services, IT telecommunications and Cloud-based infrastructure to small and mid-size companies. Managing Director Martin Haak shares how outsourcing helped Infinite Edge grow dramatically in just one year.

## The challenges

We had a lot of challenges, particularly after our first few years in business.

I'm quite technically hands on, so I found myself being responsible not only for running a business but handling

IT support requests at all hours. I was spending less and less time with my family due to late night and weekend demands.

Our customers are extremely loyal, and my wife Jules and I have built incredible relationships with our clients over the years, but we were finding many were unwilling to pay a reasonable amount for our services yet were still expecting us to be heroes and solve all of their IT problems.

All of this meant I was spending very little time on the business and almost no time on sales or reviewing customer contracts, so the business growth had stalled.

## A turning point

We thought hiring more staff would help solve some of the issues we were having. I'm not sure if we had a bit of bad luck but we weren't happy with the quality of work that was being produced.

Then I started attending MSP industry events, and was encouraged to buy PSA (professional services automation) and RMM (remote monitoring and management) tools, which we did, but the time required to set these systems up properly was taking me away from customers so these tools just became another cost.

At the end of the day we were doing all this work, spending more and more time managing people and trying to meet customer demands, and we weren't profitable. I really began to wonder what the answer was until I met James Vickery.

## Partnering with experience

It was actually one of our clients who recommended I contact James. He had worked overseas with our client, and she knew that he had experience setting up global offshore MSP teams.

I contacted James in June of 2016, and immediately saw the value. James and his team had already run and grown a successful MSP. We spoke about our technical and sales challenges, and he listened and openly shared with me some of the ways his MSP had tackled these issues.

They just got what we were going through, and so we made a decision to give it a try. Twelve months on and I no longer do technical work. I now spend my working hours on sales and paid consulting work, and finally have more time for my family.

Our company has doubled its revenue, and with the cost savings from outsourcing we became profitable and have stayed profitable ever since.

## A turnkey approach

During the initial onboarding we had lots of questions about how we would work with James's team, which were all answered quickly. They then assigned us a learning and onboarding team to get to know how we worked, what our customers expected and how our systems were designed. We provided a call script so that the team would take calls and respond to service tickets in our company name and use our company branding.

We were really surprised when they assigned us a whole team of technical and customer service staff rather than just one or two people. We went from helping our customers whenever we could find the time to giving them access to a fully staffed MSP helpdesk in a matter of days.

It was truly turnkey – we'd hired staff before who had taken weeks or months to understand our systems, but because James's team already knew how to run an MSP they had the skills to manage our clients' infrastructure and software with minimal input from us.

## Better customer experiences

A lot of things went through my mind when we were considering outsourcing. I'd had less than optimal experiences with offshore call centers from calling our Internet provider or telco, but it turned out I had nothing to worry about. The customer service was well beyond our and our customers' expectations.

Customers are happy – James and his team use Net Promoter-like scoring tools to survey the end customer, and we are consistently in the 90% range of customer satisfaction every month.

Our calls are answered every single time within two to three rings, a ticket is logged with detailed notes of the caller, and on average most incidents are resolved within the hour. If the engineer gets an unusual customer request or has any hesitation making a system change, we get a notification and can give our customer a bit of TLC if we think it's needed.

## Sustainable, healthy profit

James and his team provided us with a helpdesk and an NOC team (network operations center) that were a great help, but the real value for us has been the insightful metrics software showing how our customers were using our services. They analyzed the types of work we were doing, the frequency of the calls and number of support tickets, and the time spent on each client. They constantly share industry benchmarks as to what our customer's true monthly value should be, and that information helps us deliver services in a way that gives our clients the best outcome and ensures we are always paid for the work that we do.

This turned out to be invaluable, and it became clear why we were struggling to profit from all of our efforts. James and his team were able to identify customers who were demanding significantly more work than they were paying for, and they helped us devise a new pricing model and sales techniques that turned underperforming clients into profitable ones.

Most importantly, because the service is a pay-per-use style of service we only pay for work that we get paid for. We receive reports in real time and we can start or stop jobs or tickets depending on whether the customer is paying us for the service or if it is included in our AYCE (all you can eat) MSP contracts.

We also did our numbers and realised it was by far more cost effective to leverage James's PSA, RMM and endpoint security. We just pay for the licenses that we use, so if we obtain a new customer and need more licenses we don't have to sign lengthy contracts with the big software vendors, and this has helped us keep our costs in control and in line with our stage of growth.

We've not only doubled our revenue but we are substantially more profitable than we were 12 months ago.

## A Cloud service for people

Like a Cloud service for people, James and his team scale up or down to meet customer demand. Now Infinite Edge never has to worry about its ability to deliver on its promises.

Our goal is to double our revenue again by this time next year, and with the service in place and ready to scale up further we are now working on our strategic marketing initiatives targeting larger customers and specific verticals where we think we can add the most value.

What's great about this is I never have to worry about hiring staff or if someone has a sick day or is late for work or needs a holiday. It's not an issue we have to consider in our growth plans.

If we win a new MSP client or secure a project James can help us scale up by immediately assigning more team members, and this means all of our company focus is on marketing and business development activities, resulting in more growth and profit.

I truly feel now that we have scale we can really grow and tackle larger clients without worrying about how we're going to deliver, so outsourcing was a great decision for us. Our growth is beyond expectations and that's great, but the time I get to spend with my family has also made it a truly valuable partnership for us.

# CASE STUDY: EVISENT MSP AMPS UP

**How this Australian CEO transformed his business, increased his customer base and doubled his revenue in six months with Benchmark 365's white-label MSP**

Evisent is a fast-growing Managed Services Provider based in Melbourne, Australia specializing in IT support, strategic advice and project integration services to small and mid-market organisations.

Evisent's founder, Hayden Burt, a seasoned technology expert with a senior role as a Global Technology Manager, decided to launch the business in response to the lack of support and reliability he had encountered throughout his career from third-party IT providers. His dilemma was how to scale his business without sacrificing his commitment to great customer service. He shares below how Benchmark 365 helped him scale Evisent quickly by providing his clients with highly responsive customer and IT support, advice on winning sales techniques, and giving him the time to focus on expanding his business.

## A fresh approach

I launched Evisent to address the issue of poor service from external IT providers.

I've got a very technical background, and I've been at a senior level in the corporate world. Throughout that time I was constantly disappointed by the lack of support and assistance we'd get from third parties and IT consultants. I wanted to create an MSP that was built around relationships and great customer service. So I started Evisent as a boutique, hands-on IT service provider for companies with between 10 and 50 employees.

## The challenges

While I had a sense that our approach to IT services was different, and that we could win more clients, I was cautious about taking on too much work because it might mean that our service levels would be affected.

Our unique approach to IT advice and personalized service resulted in the business growing faster than I had anticipated. I was doing a lot of the technical work as well as sales and marketing, and it was just getting too difficult to juggle everything on my own.

I have a great relationship with my clients, and they were understanding when I wasn't readily available but it also meant that I was working all night and on weekends to keep up with demand, and I couldn't always get customer issues resolved as quickly as I had in the beginning.

To help me with the increased workload I initially thought about hiring more staff but I knew, at a minimum, I would need at least a couple of people to provide the level of expertise my customers were accustomed to. This would be a big investment at a very early stage of the business so I began hiring subcontractors. The problem was that they were rarely available right when I needed them, and they would come and go, leaving me to do the work or having to search for someone else to help me.

Ultimately, I found that managing subcontractors was becoming a job in and of itself, and it was not affording me the time or reliability I needed to focus on my business.

## A unique solution

After talking with a close friend who also ran an MSP, he suggested I speak with James Vickery, Benchmark's CEO. They had been using their team for over a year and had extremely positive things to say about them. I was incredibly nervous about outsourcing, but with so little time and so much customer demand I decided to give James a call.

The thing that I immediately liked about Benchmark 365 is that we could do a trial and that they didn't try to lock us in to a long-term contract. This suited me because I wanted to take it slow and make sure that this was a good fit for me and my business.

I was blown away by the capability. Whereas I originally thought Benchmark 365 could help with some basic support for Evisent, they in fact had a fully developed service delivery and customer service team with all of the expertise I needed to step away from IT support and to scale up the company.

## Going live

We went live with Benchmark 365 in June 2017. The onboarding process was smooth, and within a couple of weeks we had a fully scaled up team of IT support for Evisent.

The results were immediate. For one thing, the speed at which Benchmark 365 were able to answer helpdesk calls and resolve incidents was far quicker than I could do given my busy workload. Their service operates day and night, so any time our customers call or email the team are on top of it.

One of my big worries was whether our customers would refuse to work with technicians other than me, but surprisingly nobody even mentioned it. This is because I now actually spend more time speaking to my customers rather than doing the actual tech work. The relationships are stronger and the work is getting done, so they're satisfied that Evisent is delivering everything that they need.

## Better customer experiences

I'm really impressed, not just with the technical support staff at Benchmark 365 but also their administrative capability. Having a team on hand that answers the calls day and night and processes the tickets rather than me handling everything is a big advantage to Evisent and our clients.

I've noticed a big shift in the conversation with my clients: from talking just about technical issues to having positive discussions about business and strategy. They don't need me to check up on tickets or look into technical problems because Benchmark 365 is taking care of it.

I also noticed that after starting with Benchmark 365 there were fewer reoccurring incidents. I didn't anticipate them being so proactive, but the volume of support tickets has been decreasing as the Benchmark 365 team are on top of it. They let me know when something requires more than a quick fix and help me to address it.

## On-demand MSP expertise

Having a support team handling phones, tickets and projects for Evisent has been great, but what's unique about Benchmark 365 is that they actively help me find more ways to position our product offering and grow our sales.

The Benchmark 365 leadership team has been doing this for 15 years and have already been through all the pain points that my business is just starting to experience. I feel as though I could have spent years trying to gain that same experience. Instead, any time I've had a question or a problem to do with a sales issue or a tricky customer situation, the senior team are incredibly responsive and able to help guide me on what to do.

This access to senior management from an experienced MSP has totally changed the way we price, sell and deliver our services.

## Amped up for growth

I see Benchmark 365 as a permanent fixture in my company. Partnering with them is an absolute game changer for me. From day one it really revolutionized the way we operate. It reduced my stress levels and made me feel more comfortable about taking on clients rapidly.

My time has gone from spending 80% doing IT support and helpdesk and 20% of my time doing sales and strategy to a complete shift in focus. Now I spend 80% of my time marketing and selling and, as a result, we've doubled our revenue in six months, and I expect that figure to double again in the next six months.

We now have the opportunity to acquire much larger customers because I have the confidence that Benchmark 365 can handle anything I throw at them. Instead of considering hiring technicians my next hire will be an account manager, allowing me even more time to focus on Evisent's growth.

Working with Benchmark 365 is a true partnership and I would definitely recommend them to any IT business looking to grow.

Lightning Source UK Ltd.
Milton Keynes UK
UKHW011835261118
332995UK00011B/818/P